THAT DOG WILL NEVER HUNT

STORIES

John Pappas

Published by:

ORCA11BOOKS

PO BOX 17216

SEATTLE, WA 98127

ORCA11.COM

Published in the United States of America and printed on acid free paper.

First trade edition, 2010

Cover and interior graphics created and compiled by original design and through the use of stock photos and photos by contributors and the author.

The stories in this book are based on real people, dogs and events.

ISBN 978-0-578-05437-7
That Dog Will Never Hunt: stories; Pappas, John
CRS 1370355697

Author's Note

Over 40 million dogs in the U.S. live with people, and the relationships between these canines and their humans are as varied as the needs and personalities of all the folks and animals involved. Our dogs mirror our emotions and manifest them back to us in many forms. No animal has devoted so many generations trying to understand and serve us. Down through the ages dogs have known terrible cruelty at the hands of humans, as well as high esteem to the point of being silly. I have known some amazing dogs and others that, well, were less amazing but still loyal and interesting in their own way. These stories are about people and some of the ways dogs have touched their lives. I chose these stories from many collected over the years because they are all different and set in contrasting places and situations.

John Pappas, Seattle, 2010

For my brother, Chris, who has known a great dog

And for Shelley for her lifetime of caring for animals

Ackowledgments

Some stories in this book are my own and others were told to me. I would like to personally thank each person that contributed to this book by relating their personal story so I might write it down. However in the interests of privacy I must withhold their real names in most cases.

Special thanks to these good "dog people" for their thoughtful input: Jodi Woolard, Woods Creek Kennels, Monroe, WA, Stoddard Lane-Reticker, Teacher's Pet Dog Training, Avon, CT, John Kenning, Animal Rieki-Communication, Bainbridge Is., WA, Goldie Coates, Wyngold Brittanys, Bend, OR, Kent & Debbie Walker, Awreygold Retrievers, Chattaroy, WA, Rick Schloff, Seattle, WA and Mari Meehan, Rathdrum, ID.

CONTENTS

.

THAT DOG
WILL NEVER HUNT

"Just about the worst thing you can do," Jim said emphatically, adjusting his lanky frame in the booth. "She'll be nothing but a house pet." He nibbled at re-heated bacon that came with his breakfast special.

Carl nodded, mouth a serious line, waved his fork as if set to spear something flying past. "Women don't understand when they bring a huntin' dog into the house it ruins 'em. Like whackin' the nuts off a fightin' cock. Takes the hump right out of 'em." He adjusted his slouch to lean over his plate with the fork aimed between my eyes. "Sorry to have to say it, but that dog will never hunt. She'll never hold a bird."

I raised my coffee cup, mostly to avoid Carl's stern continence, and wondered if either of these guys had the first-hand knowledge to make such an assumption. Of course, knowing the dog, they might well be right. Certainly I was not an expert. Although I had hunted behind a couple of accomplished bird dogs I'd never trained one and had stopped hunting years before. Then on my birthday my thoughtful wife had surprised me with a six-week-old female Irish setter that had become an older puppy and it was decided – not by me – that the dog should be given an opportunity to perform the job programmed into her genes. It was true that Samantha's father was a field trials champion, but none of his poise had yet appeared in her. It was then my wife explained she'd gotten a special price on the pup and launched into one of those protracted explanations wives can so convincingly explore that swim exclusively within distaff logic, leaving the husband to frown at a dust bunny in the corner and nod dumbly.

"Setters, you know, as a rule they're incorrigible anyway," Jim said. "Specially the Irish. You got to accept that going in. Professional breeder told me. They've got these itty bitty pea brains and you got to limit their choices." He made a small circle with his thumb and index finger. "The brain area just ain't there. You gotta guide these dogs in respect to what to do next. Where to sleep, when to eat, where to crap. What to hunt and what critters to ignore. Otherwise, see, you've just got a idiot dog runnin' around."

"Sammy sleeps at the foot of our bed," I said, offering Carlotta a weak smile as she hurried past, a small call for help. She cast me a glance, but her mood had not been good since her fiancé' had been busted while cultivating medicinal pot on public land. Carlotta had mentioned he had a bird dog he hunted with and I may have been able to interrupt Jim and Carl to ask her if he would give me some pointers, a lateral cast to distract the censures.

I did not mention to Carl how my highly bred bird dog would ease the covers off an inch at a time during the night and roll up in them in the mode of a caterpillar reconstructing its cocoon. In the wee hours I'd wake up shivering and yank the covers back, causing Sammy to do a flip and a half and crash to the floor.

The whole subject seemed to be depressing Jim. "That time about a month ago," a nasal sigh. "Your dog got scared of something and you had to drag her out from under your pickup." He slowly shook his head while steering his spoon around the lip of his coffee cup. "I just hope you've got a leash on 'er the first time a gun goes off. Hold on tight or she'll be in the next county before the echo dies out."

"I already bought a hunting license . . ."

Carl reached over and gave my arm a reassuring pat. "Don't worry now, you just come on along with me and Corky. He's as good a little birder as there is in this valley. Season opens a week from tomorrow and I've got access to two posted fields next to orchards."

That evening after the meal, when the kids were out coaxing the last light from Indian summer, I told my wife what the guys had said regarding Samantha's future as a bird dog.

"Oh *yeah*?" she responded, instantly combat ready. "Well those two couldn't bag a bird at the *market*. And Doris told me Carl's fantasy about Corky being a hotshot pointer. The only thing that mutt's ever pointed is his food dish."

"She doesn't seem too focused . . ."

"What do you *mean*?" my wife demanded. "Sammy hunts the yard and back field like there's no tomorrow. Just yesterday she flushed a hen out of the sage on the hill. Give her a chance. Take her out after work. Work with her. You *used* to be a man of the country."

Asleep in her personal living room chair, Samantha, upon hearing her name, awoke and began unwinding long legs. As usual it was a maneuver that progressed to confused entanglement with chair arms, panic, finally falling off the chair and rolling across the rug. At eleven months she had a baseball nose, solid paws at the end of long, sinewy legs and a beautiful, rust-red coat with flowing leg feathers. Running with the kids or riding in the boat her lips and ears flapped like rags in the wind and she gazed ahead as if seeing all the way to the future, which may have been the only thing she couldn't see well enough to fear. Her latest vice was rolling in horse dung, which three baths a day couldn't dissuade her from repeating. But Sammy was my wife's baby so she would be given every opportunity to make fools of us both.

A low howl came from the kitchen. We looked where Samantha sat staring at the refrigerator. She pointed her maroon muzzle at the ceiling and uttered another mournfully melodious howl that vibrated cobwebs in the attic.

"Precious wants her ice cream," my wife said sweetly.

On Tuesday I raced home after work. There was enough light left to make the fifteen minute drive to a field I thought might hold pheasants. When we arrived, Sammy nearly knocked me over leaping out of the truck with her usual enthusiasm. But then she stopped and looked back, as if sensing this wasn't just another walk.

I pointed at a patch of weeds. "Find the birdie," I said, and a glimmer of understanding flickered in her yellow-brown eyes. She snuffled off, nose vacuuming the ground. It was about then I realized I'd pretty much exhausted my bird dog training expertise.

"The dumb leading the mad," I muttered and followed the dog into a patch of dry grass and wild wheat.

A few minutes later Sammy pointed. Well not exactly a point, more a splayed-leg stare that indicated a general direction. Containing my excitement and whispering encouragement, I moved up through clover and scrub brush. Sammy didn't move as I crept past her, atavistic blood-thirst coursing my veins. A movement to my left and a terrified mouse darted into its hole.

OK, it was a beginning.

"A mouse and a hen pheasant," my wife mused when we got home, Sammy sitting proudly between us on her skinny butt. "Not bad for a first try. She patted the boney ridge on top of the dog's narrow head. "And then she ranged a bit far?"

"About a quarter mile."

My wife cocked an eyebrow, a warning sign. "But she *came back* with feathers in her mouth. She brought those feathers right to you."

"Yes she did. It was too dark to tell if they were wild or domestic."

My wife shot me a stern look. "Of *course* they were wild. Sammy doesn't care anything about *domestic*." Right then I knew I'd better get home early for the next few nights to continue the training sessions. Student and trainer both needed it.

On opening day of bird season I declined all offers and went out alone, just Sammy and me. Let's just say our few training sessions had left me with a few doubts and it seemed prudent to begin our real hunting experience without an audience. Noble linage notwithstanding, this was a dog that adored children but had nipped a couple out of apparent confusion, panicked in the presence of strangers, chewed the left shoe of every pair I owned, continued past swats with a newspaper to gleefully treeing the neighbors' pathetic old cat and was addicted to horse dung.

Yet that quiet, bright morning it seemed to be a different dog that entered a field of corn stubble and began working back and forth as if she had some idea what she was doing. Maybe the shotgun cradled over my arm had stirred some cellular response. Every ten seconds or so Sammy would check my position, then continue her back and forth pattern, big nose moving like a hovercraft over the ridges of stubble, intruding into little thickets of slash, moving on. She even forgot to pee.

We moved across the field without incident, although there were dark hollows under the slash and broken ears picked clean that indicated birds had been here.

Near the far edge of the field Sammy suddenly contorted and froze. You couldn't call it a point in the classic sense, more a head-over-the-shoulder-eyes-rolled-back-legs-crossed position that perhaps no dog had ever before attempted. It took a minute to determine where she was indicating I should proceed. There wasn't much cover here at the end of the corn, sparse stubble with some knots of broken stalks, barely high enough for a pheasant to hunker down in. I carefully moved past the frozen dog, points of the eastern sun kaleidoscoping her bulging eyes.

A hen pheasant exploded out of the slash, then another, seemingly from ground too bare. The bright colored rooster got up last in a fury of beating wings and angry cackling. I leveled on him in a quartering-away shot, squeezed the trigger . . . missed.

Sammy was running – not in fear this time but to retrieve the downed bird, which flew strongly over a fence row and disappeared into the next field. My dog watched this, the bird's wings propelling it like a rocket, wings then locking as he glided out of sight. She stopped and looked back at me with an expression I'd see quite often over the next few years; I wouldn't call it disgust exactly.

We stood out there in the corn stubble gazing at the fence row as if expecting that bird to reappear. In her way I guess Sammy was as amazed as me. Until that moment I had never really believed in the idea of having my own bird dog, for sure I wasn't inclined to buy an expensive pup on purpose and have it professionally trained and acquire the trappings that serious bird hunters accept as basic gear. My main outdoor activity these days was fishing and Sammy liked that, except perhaps when the sandpipers took turns tormenting her. But this was a whole different thing. Sammy, it seemed, had found her competence, even if her partner was lagging a bit.

My wife met me at the door. "Well?"

I smiled and nodded.

"Aha!" she said triumphantly. "So where's the birds?"

"I missed a couple. You know, uh, it's a new shotgun and I haven't hunted for some years. My wing shooting skills are a bit rusty."

"Poor dog," my wife said, patting Sammy's neck. "You did your job, didn't you? Too bad you got stuck with somebody who couldn't hit the side of a barn with a handful of rocks."

"She was great," I said. "Well, maybe not great yet, but she got better by the hour. And you know how she's afraid of odd noises from the TV? The blast of a 12 gauge is music to her ears. There was some shooting in the next field and Sammy wanted to go help. I had to restrain her."

Later, as we were picking burrs out of Samantha's fur, my wife took a snip with the scissors on an embedded burr and asked what training techniques I had used to get her to this level.

"I told her to find the birdie."

"*And?*"

I cleared my throat. "That's pretty much the jist of it. I repeated that directive at opportune moments. She seemed to respond to that and I didn't want to confuse her with a lot of rhetoric." Avoiding my wife's piercing blue eyes, I added, "You know, in the specific sense, I've never actually trained a bird dog. Not from beginning to end. I figure if you provide them with an opportunity and a little encouragement, they either go for it or they don't. Sort of the same approach I use with women."

She punched my arm a good one.

"Sammy's doing her best and you can't even hit a bird when she finds it! Maybe you should go to the range and shoot clay pigeons or whatever. Get one of the kids to throw tin cans up in the air – no, get Jim to do it. He's expendable. You owe it to that dog to down something occasionally."

During the week the morning sessions at the restaurant with the guys pretty much centered on the bird hunt we'd arranged for Saturday. I avoided describing Samantha's first hunt, instead letting Carl drone on about Corky's locating and holding abilities. Jim seemed less enthused, frowning at the pancake he'd impaled with his fork and was flapping around the plate. He'd already been hunting with Carl and Corky during opening weekend.

"I think there's somethin' wrong with that dog," Jim muttered.

Jim's comment caused Carl's face to flush and he started waving his hands around and jabbering about Corky's prowess as a hunting dog to a degree that caused Jim to lean away and look around and Carlotta to roll her eyes at me as she filled our coffee cups.

"Tell you what," I said, causing them to pause in their arguing. "I'll meet you two at the bean field where the pipe crosses the irrigation canal at mid-morning. Say 10 o'clock." They looked at me suspiciously. "Sammy hasn't hunted with another dog before," I continued. "We'll hunt alone for a while first, so she'll be settled. She's barely started her training. You can't expect her to hunt with just anyone at this point."

Carl smirked knowingly. "Of course she's skittish, being such a young dog and a setter and all. Best thing in the world is for her to hunt with a more experienced dog like Corky.

Fastest way for a pup to learn the ropes. You'll see."

That Saturday morning I got up in the dark and sat listening to the drizzle hitting the sill outside our open bedroom window. I dressed in clean work clothes and put on my knee length rubber boots instead of my regular hiking boots. When I came back into the bedroom to say goodbye to my wife, Samantha followed and watched from the doorway.

"Ready?" I whispered.

"She's ready," my wife said sleepily, letting her hand fall on my leg. "Don't let Corky mess with her. And don't let Jim get behind you. Patty said he hunts with the safety off."

I put my thermal cup in the micro to get the coffee good and hot, found the snack in the refrigerator my wife had prepared the night before, picked up the cased shotgun in the entry.

Sammy sat alert next to me in the front seat as we made our way down quiet roads out of town. The rain quit and the promise of dawn glowed through an opening in the clouds over the river, the cab warm now, dash lights reflected in the dog's amber eyes. She was leaning forward, already hunting, staring beyond the reach of the lights where night creatures were moving. A small hawk suddenly veered in front of the truck, nearly hitting the windshield, gone as quickly as it had appeared. Sammy was unfazed. She was looking for something else in the brightening morning. Abruptly I braked. The dog tensed forward as a line of quail quick-footed through the headlights.

"I know they smell right," I said. "But we don't hunt those. Mama likes to feed them in the yard."

Moisture hung in prisms from snarled vines in the field of broken pumpkins and clumps of brown and yellow weeds had sprouted up since the harvest. A rooster pheasant called from the next field, causing Sammy's nose to go into contortions. We made our way over a deteriorated fence and moved into the muddy field.

The dog began hunting ahead 10-15 yards, snuffling back and forth, checking my position with every change of direction. I heard a hawk's whistle, a nearer croak of a red wing blackbird, the scrape of foliage against my boots and I felt a rush of contentment to have the morning and the country and an eager dog, a beautiful red dog with a nervous tail. A goofy, fearful, confused dog that is transformed here in the fields of her dreams into a skillful hunter of amazing selectiveness. She knew now we were not hunting rodents or rabbits or even quail. The single pursuit was ringneck pheasant roosters, beautiful, tough birds that might hide or run, birds that if they were people would be street gang leaders and back shooters. Sammy had locked into their scent, was well on her way to mastering a perfect point while I moved up; a thundering rise and my responsibility of a clean kill. She knew what we were hunting now and no other kind of bird could possibly distract her.

Sammy slowed and her tail began to quiver like a jalopy's exhaust pipe. Her neck stretched out, head rock steady, and she carefully raised a paw. I moved in and past her according to my roll. The rooster beat up suddenly out of a tangle of pumpkin vines and weeds, peeled off and I had to swing the gun around quickly, squeezed off a shot, saw a puff of feathers beyond the barrel. In a few leaps Sammy was on the quarry and held it until I got there. Her big teeth engulfed the bird without breaking the skin.

I let her snuffle the feathers and told her what a great dog she was, but she quickly grew impatient with accolades. She directed mad eyes at me, then quickly away, repeating this while trembling with anticipation. She only wanted to keep going.

We hunted to the end of the field and pushed two runners out ahead of us, crossed a narrow ditch and moved up into a field of mustard slash. Sammy had trouble here with the strong scent and sparse undergrowth over the furrows that allowed the birds to run. Then we worked along a small irrigation canal with thick growth on both sides. She pointed twice and I flushed three hens, which I didn't fire at, and I could see she was getting frustrated. At the end of the little canal she pushed into willows and thick cover. The dog stopped. All I could see was a small part of her back through an opening in the high weeds, but I figured she must be on point because she wasn't moving. I crept up, trying to keep the barrel of the gun away from willow branches. A young rooster exploded out of the thicket, angled fast to the left and I pulled the trigger as he went over the willows. Sammy found him dead on the other side.

The dog seemed willing to take a break. We sat there on the edge of the narrow canal and I watched her drink deeply. She drank again and raised her head, water running off her long maroon muzzle. There was a scent over there in the next field, maybe a sound I couldn't hear. Her nose twitched for awhile. She looked around to see if I was ready to go.

We had two birds and I was ready to go home. But I had agreed to meet Carl and Jim.

"Let's go find the Simpsons," I said.

It wasn't far to the 10 o'clock meeting place.

A station wagon came barreling at us ahead of a dust cloud and even before we could both stop Jim began raving out the open driver's window.

"It's been *hell*, man!" he yelled, the station wagon nearly grazing my pickup as it slid to a stop. Jim began waving an arm out the window, eyes wild. "I knew we were in trouble when Carl had to carry that stupid excuse for a dog to the car.

Picked him right up in the yard and *packed him* all the way to the car!"

"Now, now," Carl began.

Samantha leaned partly across me to stare out the window at these people making all the commotion. In the cargo area of the station wagon Corky the Springer spaniel cowered over the spare tire, eye whites glowing like snake-eyed dice through the fogged window.

"You don't mean Carl's Corky?" I asked. "Corky, the bird dog?"

"That's not even the beginning! Sonofabitch went crazy over at Anderson's field! Allergic to cows or nettles or something. We had to pack him all the way back and lock him in the wagon." Jim grimly shook his head. "Big mistake. *Real big* mistake."

"Not nettles," Carl corrected. "I told you he can't abide certain types of goats and Anderson has those weird imported goats from Scotland or somewhere. Just because a bird ran across the road you got trigger-happy. I said we shouldn't stop. It's your fault Corky had an olfactory episode."

"I'd like to give him a permanent olfactory episode!" Jim screamed at Carl. "He totally messed up Patty's car! Ate the damn insulation right out from around the windows!" Jim swung his head back in my direction. "You ever heard of that? Huh? A dog nibblin' the rubber right off from around the windows!"

"Now, now," Carl said.

"That *still* ain't all, " Jim said through gritted teeth. "Then wonder dog back there puked and crapped all over the back. And it wasn't solid ejection, *you know what I mean*? It flowed and seeped down into the lower compartment, man. Look at him back there – shakin' like a goose layin' a football! *Don't you understand I can't have this stinking puking animal in Pat-*

ty's car." Jim seemed to focus on me then.

"You have a canopy with a lockable door."

"No way," I said. "Other than that, how was the morning hunt?"

"Thank you so much for – *never mind.* How'd you do?"

"We have a couple of birds. Thought I'd head on home for a late breakfast."

"Not a chance," Jim replied. "I'll blow out your tires. Ding-bat dog's gotta save the day."

"Whoa." I looked at Sammy. "Did you hear that? Could you hunt for somebody that addressed you in such a manner?"

"Alright-*alright,*" Jim said. "What do I have to do? Please, superdog, for God's sake hunt for us. I'll buy you a steak."

Sammy and I looked at each other, our noses inches apart. A tiny feather clung to the edge of her nostril. She burped. I looked back at Jim. "Sammy says if you'll shut up she'll give it another hour."

The next hour didn't go much better for Corky. We pried him out of the back of Jim's station wagon and he tried. But twice he sniffed his way past hidden birds and Sammy pointed them. One was a rooster that Jim downed on his third and last shot, firing away like a tail gunner. Corky watched the excitement with wet eyes and a droopy expression. Pats on the head and whispered encouragement didn't cheer him much, although he welcomed the sympathy. He was one of those willing little Springers with the yen but not quite the natural ability and had never received the right training. Still, he kept trying, following Sammy now.

"He's in a regressed state because of the goats," Carl confided. "And because that asshole Jim keeps bullying him. Jim never hunted at all, you know, until I took him out. Acts like he knows about hunting and dogs. He never had a hunting dog. Doesn't know the first thing about dogs. That thing he's got at home doesn't even qualify as a dog. Stubby little back-biter, that's all he is. Get your heel yet?"

"He's tried," I admitted. "He's pretty sneaky all right. Strange little dog."

"Jim says he wasn't like that before Patty got him clipped. As if he knows what's been done and he blames all male people. He doesn't like Jim much anymore either. Course they had to do something. More than one neighbor threatened to shoot the randy little bugger."

When I didn't answer Carl continued. "I'd appreciate you not judging Corky on the basis of today's performance. He's really a very good bird dog."

"I'm sure he is. Springers are great bird dogs."

"Yes they are." Carl nodded firmly. "It is true Corky has had the occasional problem with certain types of goats. Foreign ones. Not American goats. Hybrid foreign goats. I've been told by reliable people that it's a case of olfactory perversion – a violent reaction to certain unfamiliar smells. And his is not an isolated case. But that little dog's had some good days, very good bird days, and he's experienced. I'm sure he could teach your young dog a lot."

"Maybe so," I said. "But for now I'm kind of sold on Sammy finding her own way."

"What do you mean?" Carl asked, incredulous. "She's just a pup. A flighty pup."

"Um-hm. But I think she's remembering some things her daddy knows. And I think I should just follow her around for a while."

Carl's wavering eyes seemed to squeeze closer together at the apex of his long, ridged nose and I was pretty sure the conversation was ended and that it was doubtful there would be another conversation with Carl right away about bird dogs, which was fine with me.

Watching the two dogs together, I marveled that Sammy didn't seem to mind that Corky was struggling with the residue from some kind of episode, or that he often got in her way, and she wasn't frightened that relative strangers were coming over her on point. Sammy hunted like she'd been doing it for generations, and I guess she had.

Just before noon I said, "We have to head in now."

"We're short of a limit," Jim complained.

"Then let Corky find it for you," I said. "Give him a chance."

That afternoon after he'd finished hunting Jim stopped by my house. I was sprawled on the couch with sock feet on the coffee table, drowsily reading a magazine. When my wife answered the door Sammy jumped between Jim and her and barked ferociously, lots of big, wet, flashing teeth. No way was Jim coming in until I went to the door and calmed the dog.

"She's very protective around the house," I said, as Jim sidled inside.

"She has a gentle mouth," my wife said pleasantly. "Her fangs usually stop short of bone."

Jim winced and headed for the living room while I went to the kitchen to get us some coffee.

When I came into the living room Sammy was sitting in front of Jim, staring at his every move, leaning forward a little as if ready to spring.

"What's got into your dog?" Jim asked uneasily. "We were just hunting together – now she looks like she's ready to attack me."

I handed him a cup of coffee. "For one thing, you're sitting in her chair."

"*Her* chair. Oh. Well. I don't mind moving." Jim slid out cautiously and onto the couch.

Sammy crawled up on her chair, wrapped long legs around

the arms possessively, uttered a satisfied groan and settled into glaring at Jim.

Jim bent close to me and whispered, "Why doesn't she like me?"

I considered Jim's question. "It could be a professional critique." I said.

"What's that supposed to mean?" Jim demanded.

"Well, you belittled Corky in front of everybody, which made him feel worse. And you yelled at Carl when Sammy was on point, causing the bird to get up early. Then you missed those two easy shots over Little Canal. She remembers those things."

Jim was speechless, though his mouth seemed to be trying to form words.

I sipped some coffee and Samantha and I leaned back and smiled at each other.

LITTLE STAR LAKE

Accepting total blame for a crime you did with a friend can be the fortified wine of a guilty conscience, like a penitent wino reflecting through the alleys of his past. It's less permanent than giving up a kidney to a needy buddy, but on those nights when you can't sleep and finally knock yourself out wino style it can get you through the night; that pretty much describes the cycle I rode for years.

My parents bought a cabin on the shore of this northern Wisconsin lake and we started coming here nearly thirty years ago, when I was about the size of an armload of firewood. Little Star isn't much as lakes go in this part of the country: fishing seldom better than fair, August mosquitoes the size of hummingbirds, and in mid-winter you better wear a ski mask with your parka unless you don't care if your nose remains in the center of your face. The few cabins and houses around our side of the lake, opposite the town by a scant mile, are well-spaced and no one is sure where one property ends and their neighbor's begins. My parents and the rest of our family still enjoy part of the summer here, but I come much more often, even in winter, since the work I do for Dad involves tracts of timber in the area. I stretch the work out since there are people here I like being around, and in this typically rural by-gosh-friendly-but-narrow small lake community everybody knows your name, even if you preferred some of them didn't.

The war had been officially over for a few years, most of the local boys made it home, euphoria had given way to rural depression, and new people were blamed at least in part for whatever needs were not being met. Some folks lumped Billie Skelly in with new people because she had stayed away sixteen years, and perhaps because she reappeared with a fourteen year old boy and a man from Texas by the name of Conrad Jasper who was not the boy's biological father. (Not that Billie had discussed this with anyone, but around here folks know the last time your shadow passed by Minor Lervold's Saloon.) She had come back to claim her birth home after her father, Burton, was crushed inside his old Ford pickup when it intercepted a train near the Minaqua station. Now there were people that insisted the signal had malfunctioned, which it certainly did from time to time and I was one of those who had observed a failure, but it was also known that Burton's hearing and eyesight were failing.

The Jaspers resided next to our property and had assumed the role of looking out for the Case girls while their parents were away, a common occurrence. Brenda Case had some kind of roving librarian job and Paul was a sharpener for sawmills. And the Cases trusted Billie since she had been the girls' baby sitter when we were all much younger.

Most of us, even our local sheriff, had less total accrued community time than Billie, her last name now Jasper, hard to reconcile since she so resembled her father, Burton Skelly, who built his modest house overlooking the lake after the previous, previous war, the most recent previous having delivered us to the present cold war which was steadily warming. I say modest because he never installed central heating or cared much about inside plumbing (even our cabin had been upgraded with a septic system), but he built a square, solid structure with stone fireplace and chimney and two small bedrooms upstairs under the steep gables. The hand pump for bringing up good well water is right outside the kitchen door and it's only a few steps to the garage and shop where his canoe and tools still reside; beyond the shop stands the plank outhouse, complete with quarter-moon cutout in the door.

Burton married a Chippewa woman he called Truffle, and she had Billie about five years before my father purchased the angular two acres next door, between Burton's and Rudy Birkenstock's property. Rudy and his wife, Corella, run a sort of resort during the summer for less than well-heeled families that venture up from the cities. In front of their house are two cabins they let out by the week. There are several small boats for rent, too, and a dock with a swimming ladder. If demand required it the Birkenstocks would let out their house and temporarily move into a little camping trailer next to the goat pen. They kept goats for the milk, which Corella believed essential in controlling her mental malady. We didn't see much of Corella.

Burton doted on Billie, but he wanted a boy and they kept trying. After several miscarriages Truffle left one winter morning – strangely enough I happened to see her going into the woods without her snowshoes and wondered if something was wrong. It had begun snowing again and I knew her rabbit snares must be buried, they had plenty of wood, so what could be her purpose? I was only fourteen but had been Burton's student for some time and was acquiring a sense about the woods.

Burton and I found her the next day under low-sweeping pine branches, her skin the color of snow against dark hair and brows, clutching a doll her father had made for her when she was a child. It was generally assumed she felt useless for not producing a boy, a belief I resisted since I so admired Burton. On numerous occasions he had in some way helped everyone around our lake and I refused to believe he could be responsible for Truffle's apparent suicide. He was from eastern Kentucky originally, served in Europe during the war, and somehow ended up here directly after being discharged. He liked red-white-blue suspenders, carried a hunting knife on his belt and in summer usually wore buckskin moccasins. His prowess as a hunter was legendary. There were stories of game wardens surrounding his house at night when they were certain he had a deer down out of season. He would slip out in his moccasins, quarter the deer in the dark woods, and make several trips home with the meat while the wardens sat out in the brush waiting for him to make a move.

Anyway, that afternoon, shortly after I'd arrived, I thought something might be wrong when I looked up from my desk to see Conrad Jasper trudging up the path with chest out and floppy Stetson set straight on his large head. A man on a mission. At his knock I opened the door quickly, surprising him, a small pleasure.

"I'm here to inquire if you actually saw the soldiers?"

"What soldiers?" There was a tightening in my gut, like when you hear a sound in the night you can't identify.

"The ones visited the Case girls," He glanced back in the direction of the red house a long stone's throw beyond Burton's place. "Brenda and Paul are not at home," he said in a low, cautionary way.

I tried to appear disinterested, looking past Conrad to a snow-laden pine branch in my yard. "Well, Con," I said, drawing it out to match his drawl, emphasizing his nickname, Con, an oxymoron since he could never make a living as one. "I did see three G I's on our road earlier today, just as I drove in. And I did wonder what their business might be since there was no apparent defensive need."

"No," Con said firmly, staring at me along his eminent nose. "It was not Army business. They went to the Case's."

"And you being here means there could be something suspect about their visit."

"They came," Con said gravely, "to take advantage of the girls. And I'm asking around to see who saw what. Such as the fight with the straggler."

"Fight?"

"Well," Con said, clearing his throat so his jowls vibrated, "there was some unusual sounds, so, in regards to our responsibility, Billie and mine, you know, with the girls, I went over there. I intercepted the last one out. But when I tried to question him he resisted. So I had to restrain him some." Con moved his large head side to side. "Resisted." He looked up quickly. "Did you happen to see anything?"

"I thought I saw someone on the bank head down to the lake." I peered around him, beginning to feel the stale chill of desperation. "I doubt they tried the ice. It's not good yet."

"That was one of 'em got away. Two made it out the back and ran down the bank. Third one's at Case's. The girls are watching him."

Watching him? "What actually happened?" I asked, grabbing up a pair of shoe packs near the door and pulling them on over my woollies.

"I think," Con said gruffly, "that Veronica for sure was

raped. Maybe Bonnie. We're not entirely sure yet about Bonnie. The one I caught said he'd been invited to the house by Veronica when she went to that dance at the school gymnasium last night." Con glanced toward the Case house. "Lying punk."

"Maybe Ronnie did invite them," I said.

Conrad reared back, pale eyes wide. "That's a damn dirty thing to say. She's a nice girl."

"Sure she is." I was making an effort to keep my voice even. "She's also eighteen and built like a royal brick shit house and so's her sister." I knew it sounded wrong, like my voice, but I didn't care now.

Conrad's arms curved away from his thick body, a gigantic bird ready for flight. "I guess it's true what they say about you – a man of your age talking about neighbor girls that way. I can see why some people –"

"Hey!" I took a step toward him. I wasn't as wide as Con, but we were about the same height. "How did they find their way here? How the hell did they know?"

His look changed to bewilderment. I finished tying the rawhide bootlaces and brushed past him. As we approached the Case house I saw through the front window Billie's son, Tommy, standing in the living room. The new boy, Tony, was in the unheated foyer, his dog waiting just outside. Tony boarded with the Jaspers; his mother, an attractive woman, worked over in the next town at the Minaqua Hotel-Restaurant and lived, I was told, in an upstairs hotel room.

"What're you doin' here?" Con demanded.

"Came with Jimmy," Tony said, eyes fixed on the ground in front of his boots.

"Well, get your butt outta here," Con commanded. "Nobody asked for your help. Go on."

Tony shuffled across hard snow and we entered the house.

Con appraised the living room, his gaze lingering on Tommy standing there looking somewhat embarrassed, the girls huddled together on the couch. They were fully dressed in plaid shirts over their pullovers and jeans, regular winter clothes. Bonnie had her hands cupped over Veronica's who was quietly sniffling. I nearly went to her, caught myself and even took a small step back.

Con frowned at the girls. "Where is he?"

"They let him go," Tommy said.

Con's attention turned to his stepson, a tall, angular lad with big hands and a sour mouth. "Let him go?" Con repeated.

Tommy nodded emphatically. "Let him go."

Bonnie flung her sister's hands aside and stood defiantly, started yelling at Con. "He's gone and good riddance! All gone! And I hope you follow him!"

"Now listen here young lady –"

"Nobody *asked you* to meddle in our business. My Dad even said he was in Texas once and he didn't like it. Not one bit! Why are you even *here?*"

"You darned well know your daddy Paul asked me to keep an eye on things while he was away. That's what we do around here. The people of Little Star Lake look out for one another. And don't think he won't hear about your behavior when it comes –"

"Oh, put a sock in it," Bonnie said, freckles and nostrils flaring, "you aren't from here. You're from another country. *Texas.* Where they beat their women and love their longhorns." She started past and Con grabbed her arm. I felt my muscles tighten as she grimaced from his powerful grip, but before I could react Bonnie got in his face and started spitting out words.

"Go ahead! Beat on me too. That's what you do, right?

Beat on people. Seems like that's about *all* you can do." Her tearful blue eyes held a defiant glare.

Con relaxed his grip slightly and she twisted free, grabbed her fur-trimmed parka off a peg and stalked out, slamming the door.

Large face flushed with anger and confusion, Con moved closer to Veronica who sat staring into the twisted handkerchief in her hands. "We're just here to help," Con said, fingering his hat as if he was thinking about taking it off. "And I have to ask if you need any, you know, medical attention? I can get the car started and take you into town if you need to see the doctor."

"No." Veronica looked up at the three male faces staring at her. "*Please*, I don't need *anything. Nothing happened.*" She made a quick dab at her nose with the handkerchief and shot me a resentful look.

"I would appreciate it if you would all just go now," she said, sounding more in control. "Get your kicks somewhere else. This is stupid." She dropped her head, causing the V of her flannel shirt to expose some cleavage. Tommy shifted and cocked his head.

"I think she has a right to be alone now, if that's what she wants." I asked Veronica if that was what she wanted, for the benefit of Con and Tommy.

"*Yes.* For God's sake, Jerry's probably out there lost in the woods." She looked up with narrowed eyes. "About the last thing I want now is more male drivel. Just go."

I took a step toward Con, aware of Tommy still staring at Veronica. "She wants us to leave," I said firmly. I went to the door, opened it, waited expectantly. It took a few seconds, but they filed out. We went through the foyer and started across the parking area with islands of slick, thin layers of packed snow. Bonnie stood over on the edge of the bank above the lake, Tony next to her, his dog between them. They just stood looking out at the frozen lake.

"*Hey*," Con yelled. They turned toward us. "I thought I told you to get the hell home."

Boy and dog began walking slowly along the crest of the bank, heads down.

I didn't say what first came to mind. "I could use Tony's help," I said reasonably. "We could check out the woods. That soldier might still be around."

"Prob'ly half way back to the base by now," Con replied angrily. "Punk coulda made the highway and hitched a ride in no time. They'll pick up anybody wearin' the brown."

"How would he know where the highway is?" I stepped in front of Con. "You don't have any problem with me and Tony having a look, do you?"

"What the hell's the point? He's gone."

"Or half froze. Weather report said five above tonight. You want that on your conscience?"

"Ah, hell. Mighta known you'd mess it up. They say you're about half commie anyway."

"Yeah, and the other half pervert. Everything they say about me is true. So you got any objection regarding Tony and me looking for this guy?"

"Go ahead, then, take the kid. Maybe you'll both freeze out there." He gave me a mean look. "I won't come lookin'. I'm washin' my hands of the whole matter right now. But that don't mean I don't have my eye on you."

Con stalked off and I yelled at Tony. He stopped and looked back. "C'mon," I yelled, waving an arm. "I need your help."

He stared, turned to watch Con as he tramped toward Burton's house, then he and the dog began running in my direction.

"Wes?" I turned and Veronica motioned me back into the

house. I turned toward her as Tony and the dog ran up. Bonnie was coming along too, ready to return now that Con had left.

"Ronnie wants to tell me something," I said. "You talk to Bonnie a minute."

I kicked snow off my boots again and entered the house. Barely inside the door, but out of sight of anyone outside, Veronica put her arms around my waist and rested her cheek against my chest. I placed a hand lightly on her back.

"Let them go," she whispered. "I don't want to see any of them again."

"What the heck happened? Did you invite those boys here?" I tried to sound casual, but then she bent her head back and gave me a look of strange amusement that felt like a punch in the gut.

"What difference does it make?" she said.

Snow had come and gone, then it got colder and more snow fell. The new snow was only a few inches deep and where the sun penetrated the forest there were bare spots. I needed time to calm down. That was the real reason I offered to go looking for this guy. I didn't really want to find him. I didn't want to talk to anyone right then.

A hundred yards into the woods I was already feeling better. We altered our path whenever necessary to walk in the soggy, bare patches between still-fragrant pine. We favored narrow animal trails that led us over snowy spots dividing carpets of rotting leaves from the maples and poplar, a mix of oak and dulled, hot-colored leaves from wild nut trees, the graceful long yellows from birch. This was mine too, these changing woods, like the Lake-of-a-Thousand-Faces I had only to lift my eyes from whatever work was on my desk to let flow into my thoughts.

Fresh tracks in a large patch of snow caused me to stop. I looked around, took a slow breath. Crisp air brought the smells of the woods sharply alive. The dog and boy were watching too, standing quietly, the way you should be in the woods unless there is reason to make sounds. It pleased me that I could take some credit for this. Most of my life had been spent in Wausau; not exactly the urban jungle, but not like being here with the feel of real winter coming and restless animals. My father had taught me what he could about the woods – Burton had taught me how to be part of them. And I'd passed along what I could to this strange, dark-haired boy from the coast that had landed here as if from space, had landed complete with local dog that never left his side, a dark caramel border collie that had been acquired – through Tony's mother's request and payment I'd heard – by the Jaspers for the boy. This dog seemed unusually aware of what people expected of it, and was in fact from a Johnson's stock dog's litter, which folks around here would stand in line and pay hard-earned money for. They must have let Billie have the pup out of respect for Burton.

"Who was that came by?" I said.

Tony moved a little past me and bent to examine the tracks. "Bobcat." He looked up with a grin. "Pretty fresh. In no hurry."

"What do you suppose he was doing here?"

The boy frowned, looked around. "Maybe the Case's chickens. Or the Birkenstock's chickens. They have a baby goat, too."

"When the snow gets a little deeper this cat might try for the goat. Chickens are fair game anytime." I pointed toward a set of rabbit tracks disappearing into a thicket. "See how he circled that brushy place. He knows mister rabbit lives in there and wants to check his front and back door. If he gets a chance at him in the open he'll know how to head him off."

"Do you think he'll come tonight?"

I shrugged, feeling some satisfaction at being considered an expert woodsman by this boy.

"Where do you suppose that soldier boy ran to?" I said, thinking about other matters now.

The boy crouched down to stroke the dog and stare into the woods. Without looking up he said, "Skip thinks he could be at the spring."

Of course he would say the spring. Barely a mile from my cabin and I'd never known it was there until he led me to it over a month ago to tap some of the biggest maples you can imagine. How could he have found it so quickly when I'd been exploring these woods since I was a kid? We'd been tapping most of the afternoon and he was learning about spout angle and where to bore, and I had mentioned taking care not to run the trees dry, and he'd said there were several big maple trees at the spring.

"Why in the world do you think he would be at the spring?" I asked.

"Well, if he stumbled onto it, maybe he'd want to stay there awhile." The boy's dark eyes were intent. "There's shelter under the trees," he said. "And water. It's a place to stop and think things out."

I suppose I smiled a little, because he did. "Let's have a look then." I thought it would be a good way to pass time while pretending to be doing something.

When Tony had told me about the spring he referred to it as "pretty," which he immediately corrected to "a good place to hole up." But it *was* a pretty spot in the deep woods, a lush indentation of perfect dark-green browse and an assortment of trees around a small pool of crystal water that came bubbling out of the ground and flowed no more than ten yards before disappearing again. The animal tracks around the water were defined and un-busy, as if they had come gently to this place.

As we approached I heard a muffled cough, causing me to come to attention. Then I noticed tracks. We continued a few steps until the boy pointed. Under the low-sweeping branches of a pine a dark shape that didn't fit. It moved slightly; a leg.

As we came closer, I said, "We aren't here to cause you harm. Are you all right?"

"Get away from me," a hoarse voice answered.

"You don't want to freeze to death. Come out and talk."

"Go to hell."

"The girls don't blame you for anything at this point," I said. "Come out and explain yourself and we'll see what we can do about getting you out of this."

"I've got a knife."

"And if you use it what then? You either get an ass whippin' or you make it worse for yourself. Now get out here. And I better not see a weapon."

A few seconds of quiet. The dog was sniffing to catch this stranger's scent, but staying put.

A marked up face with streaks of dried blood poked out of the snowy pine branches. "You better step aside, mister." He raised the knife, a commando type. "I've taken all the shit I'm gonna from you crazy hicks."

"Didn't come to give you any," I said, stepping ahead of the boy. "Unless you really deserve it. Do you?"

"Hell no!" the young man blurted, eyes wild. He stepped clear of the branches, kept the knife up. He looked athletic, had a PFC stripe and hair long enough to separate him from a recruit, but not from a real vet. He was a nice looking kid, bruised face full of anger.

I realized I was getting mad too. "Did you guys force Veronica and Bonnie to do anything they didn't want to do?"

"Not a bit!" he said fiercely. "We had a couple beers. Danced a little. Then Bonnie started tryin' to sing like Billy Holiday. Then Ronnie asks me to go in the bedroom to see somethin'. So I went."

"She asked you to go into the bedroom."

"Yeah. We hadn't hardly got started and then that big man came crashin' through the door. He was yellin' and swingin'. Chas and Darryl, they ran out the back. So when I came out of the bedroom he started beatin' on me."

"So you're Jerry."

The young man blinked. "Guess I been singled out for some reason. But I ain't taking no more. That crazy sonofabitch caught me with a couple, but no more." Jerry raised the knife.

"Where would your buddies have headed?"

Jerry glanced around. "Same way I'm headed. And you're in the way."

I shook my head. "First we'll go back to the Case's. We'll get everything straight. Then I'll drive you back to the base."

"Not on your fucking life!" He raised the knife a little higher.

This wasn't how I thought it would go. I guess I hadn't really thought about what might happen if I found the guy. I took another step. The dog uttered a low growl.

"Kid," I began, trying to sound calm. "I don't think you understand the situation. This is a proper little tight-ass community. The word rape has been brought up."

"No!" Jerry looked around wild-eyed. "She asked –"

"Doesn't matter what you say at this moment," I interrupted, letting some anger in. "What the girls say. What that big guy says. Me. What this boy says, even what his dog says, it all takes precedence over anything you might tell me in the next five seconds. So if I say to come with me and clear this thing up before it gets any worse, what do you think the smart thing to do would be? That is if you're innocent of the charge that's been put up against you."

Jerry's face went through some contortions. Then he came.

I have to admit, I wasn't ready. Before I could take a set he was charging and swinging the knife and though I deflected his thrust it caused a foot to slide in the snow and I lost my balance. He ripped the knife back and the blade sliced through the parka and into my arm, knocking me flat on my back. He fell on top of me, raging, plunged the knife at my face – I managed to twist enough so it dug sharp pain into my shoulder.

Jerry screamed then, pitching back. I came up and saw the dog with his teeth buried in Jerry's calf, Jerry slashing with the knife. The boy was jabbing a pine limb at him while the dog hung onto his leg. I gained my feet and launched myself at Jerry. We ended up in a pile with me punching and hoping to get a grip on Jerry's throat with my good arm. He'd lost the knife as he hit the ground, but he kicked free of us and scrambled up, crashed off through the woods, the dog in pursuit.

The boy said the dog's name and he came back immediately. I could see the blood oozing out the cut sleeve of my parka and felt a dull pain in my shoulder. I pulled the boy to me, checking his clothes. He resisted.

"Skip's bleeding," he said. The dog limped into the small space between us and seemed to be checking the boy like I had been doing. There was blood on his back and one side of his muzzle.

"I'm all right," the boy said, impatient. He noticed my shoulder. "You're bleeding in two places. I'll get you a stick."

"I can walk OK," I said.

"In case he comes back."

Oh that. The boy looked a little scared, but determined. I nodded and he picked up the dead pine limb he'd used for a weapon. He put one end up on a log and jumped on the small end until it broke to walking stick length. He watched me get to my feet. I felt dizzy and decided to stand still a minute or two. I accepted the stick; one end had a knot the size of a baseball bat. I had worked a handkerchief up under my parka to the bloody shoulder wound. The cold air was helping with coagulation of the arm wound.

"Skip can make it back," the boy said.

I looked at him and realized it was a question. "Skip's a good dog." I looked at the spring bubbling out of the ground in such perennial fashion, then studied the trail. I decided I could make it too.

The doctor had given me a shot against possible infection and as an afterthought something for the pain. I had just taken the second dose of the pain stuff in half the time recommended on the bottle, but I was beginning to feel better. Two candles well behind me and a few flickers from the crackling stove seemed about right. Beyond the window the lake was a mottled blanket of ice and white that ended at the dark line of trees. It looked as dreamy and mysterious as when I'd first seen it as a child. Pour a little wine and watch the show. In a town or city you can press your cheek against window glass and as far as the angle allows see pavement, storefronts, traffic, people . . . this was better.

On our lake there's very little light after 9 pm. Same with the town on the other side of the water – no sense lighting up the countryside in the middle of the night when decent folks are supposed to be asleep. A fresh snow shower, now clear sky and full moon makes for perfect viewing. Bright moonlight on frozen lake, shooting stars against sky so black it's like looking into a giant inkwell full of tiny lights. Over in the little bay a deer's shadow moving onto the white. A red fox much closer, checking around one of Birkenstocks' cabins for scraps left by long gone tourists. The beginning of the hard season for the animals. At night you see urgency in their shadowy movements and respect their commitment to survival as life's responsibility. Wood crackles in the stove and you feel the cold outside. You think about who you are. Why you are. Why you absolutely love some people and not others, at least not in the way they love you. Which leads to the question of why anyone should love you.

Just two days ago, the day before coming up to the lake, I had broken off a relationship with a young woman Dad had recently described as ideal in every way. Ideal in every way. Her family, education, church, intelligence, manners, willingness to procreate, all lined up like the lists my mother uses to guide her daily activities. It hadn't always been this way, but Dad had been fortunate in business. Throw in a little luck regarding timber leases and a thirty-fold increase in some penny mining stock and we were a mini-dynasty in the making. It changed my parent's perspective of the world. In the case of Annette he had been hopeful, and perhaps I had been too. She was pretty, no particularly annoying habits beyond a fervent interest in the really rich and burping after a meal. She was twenty-five and pragmatic about using precautions during sex. She always tried to be accommodating. Maybe that was the problem.

No, that wasn't the problem.

There was a soft knock on my door. I was pretty sure it was the one I had been hoping for and dreading. I rose unsteadily, tottered across the room, opened the door and the cold rushed in. I looked beyond the shrouded head where

Tony's dog sat watching. "Is Skip with you?"

"He met me on the way over," Ronnie said. "I guess he's still edgy about what happened today. You know how he looks out for the kid and all of us."

Between pine bows the second floor window of Burton's house was illuminated by candlelight and I made out the pale shape of a face behind the glass. Tony was still awake. Looking out a window like I had been doing. Watching his dog guard Ronnie on her way to my place. How many times had he watched this?

"Aren't you going to invite me in? Or does your arm in a sling make it too difficult?"

I ignored the sarcasm and pushed the door wide, but she just stood there.

"Wait, Skip." I went to the table and took the spoon from the bowl of vegetable soup I'd started an hour ago. I reached into the sack of dog food next to the refrigerator and grabbed a handful of nuggets, dropped them into the soup bowl. I turned the porch light on and took the bowl outside, put it down near the top step. The dog came up the stairs cautiously, began lapping at the bowl. There was a crude bandage on his right foreleg. The fur around the wound on his side had red streaks running out from it but no bandage.

"So you two are the heroes of the day," she said quietly.

"He sure is." I glanced at her face illuminated by the yellow porch light, feared looking at her too directly. She had pushed the parka hood back so her dark hair tumbled out and framed her face.

"The porch light is on."

"I don't care." She flashed a defiant smile. "Did the doc give you a tetanus shot?"

"Yeah. Who tended Skip's wounds?"

"Tony. Con said dogs just lick their wounds to make them

well. Don't have to do anything. Bonnie helped the kid with a bandage and some Mercurochrome. He insisted he had to do something."

"Dog saliva is just one more thing Con doesn't know crap about," I said.

"I didn't think that dog would take the Mercurochrome, but he did. Just moaned a little with his head down while Tony painted it on the gash. So why don't you pick up the bowl and turn the stupid porch light off and we'll all move inside?"

"Don't pick on me, I'm medicated."

"Then just do what I said. It will all become clear."

Bowl in hand, I had to coax the dog into the cabin. From midsummer, whenever I was here, I'd been slipping him food at night. He came out of the shop where he slept to take food or scraps of meat I would put down on the steps. But he would not come into my house unless tempted with something like homemade maple syrup on a piece of wheat bread. I knew Skip's linage, his parents and grandparents, their dedication to people and stock, yet I had never been around a dog like this on a daily basis. Here he did not have the routine of taking care of stock, so the boy became his charge. In extension his responsibility included the people that lived in the immediate vicinity, the herd, of which I was a privileged member.

"You love that dog, don't you?"

She had taken off the heavy coat and poured a glass of red wine from the bottle on the counter, tossed it off, was refilling the glass. She turned on the small light over the sink.

"He always seems to know what to do," I said. "That is something you have to admire. At least I do. He sure saved my butt today."

"He's a Johnson dog," she said, settling it. "So now what?"

I didn't answer, watching the dog clean up the last of what was in the bowl.

"I'm really tired of this game. I really don't care for any more of this."

I turned and looked at her, the glint of wine on her lower lip, thought about what she was saying, what she might be feeling. When I'd stumbled out of the woods she had come running, but I whispered caution and she had restrained herself like always, good scout, loyal secret companion. Rudy Birkenstock appeared and led me to his car. I wouldn't even let her ride along to the doctor's office.

"Want to hear about it?"

I nodded. Not that I wanted to, but she had every right to tell me.

"We were at the dance and it was fun. Bonnie had on one of my dresses and her eyes were big as dollars. And boy, was she getting the looks." She paused to let this sink in.

"But then she has virtually no *experience*. That's the important thing, right? There were all these young guys away from home, all these girls with no certifiable *experience*. None of the soldiers knowing what orders would come next." She gulped some wine, continued giving me a crooked smile that had nothing to do with humor.

Her silence became a lead weight in the room. I thought about asking her to slow down on the wine because she wasn't used to it. But it wasn't for me to tell her anything. The dog and I would see that she got home. That reminded me of the dog. He was over by the door, looking uncomfortable. I went to let him out.

"You love me too," she said so quietly I paused, wondering if I'd actually heard it.

The dog lay down in a bare spot next to the steps. I shut the door carefully and went back to the table, sat and looked across at her beautiful face framed by all that hair highlighted by candlelight, graceful hands around the glass, dark eyes downcast now, the V of her shirt exposing olive skin. Funny, I thought, Bonnie's so blonde and freckly. I saw Ronnie at twelve diving with perfect form off the rough diving platform her father had built and we had all helped move out into six feet of water so the top would be two feet above the lake. I'd been ashamed of my thoughts about her then, this kid buddy I carried around on my shoulders. This kid I'd taught to swim near the same reed bed where I had learned.

"You always have," she said, sad eyes not seeing. "But I guess what you need to hear is what *exactly* happened. For the scoreboard. The *experience*. So. The deal is he wanted me to go into the bedroom with him and I went. And we made out some. And he pawed me some. And then we were on the bed with our pants down and he was primed as a hot water pump." I heard the wine going in the glass, did not look over there.

"His skin was hot and so was mine – are you picturing this? – and he started inside me and I changed my mind. Sorry, would rather not. Of course he didn't take this well. So he got a little violent. But I was jumping around . . . anyway, what happened was he messed up my jeans which I was trying to pull up."

There was the dog to consider, if he went back to the shop. There was the crust that would be on the snow in the morning after a clear, cold night like this, how distinctly it separated the old from new tracks so you knew which animals had moved. There was the possibility of one or both of the elder Case's coming home to tend their progenies.

"About then," she said, "Con came rushing in and the other two went out the back door. Jerry stumbled out of the bedroom just in time to get his ass beat by the gallant Texan. I guess that's about it, unless you'd like more details. Would you like more details?"

I shook my head. After a gloomy silence I glanced over and saw a wet reflection on her cheek, jaw set. She was determined not to make a sound.

"The sheriff?"

"Yeah," she said hoarsely. "After Birkenstock ran you into the doc's Sheriff Kune drove out in his jeep and tried to ask the right questions, but Bonnie and me convinced him Con had been drinking and started the whole thing. We said he scared us more than the soldiers. Kune went to have a talk with Con. You were home then, you must have heard Billie screaming and ranting all the way to my house."

"I did think I heard some jays fighting."

"Anyway," she continued, "I don't think the Jaspers will be bothering us anymore, except maybe for that creep Tommy. Maybe I should add to my experience with him. Carve a notch on the ol' bedpost for hot li'll Tommy. Do I have your go-ahead?"

"I'm sorry."

"So am I," she said. "Sorry I let you put me in your guilt trip. Sorry I believed you about experience and I'd see the world was really my oyster and you'd be some barnacle on the ass of childish horny dreams."

She laughed suddenly and her wine glass fell off the table, landed on my slipper, rolled off and made a half circle on the floor.

"So at least I got your eyebrows up with that one," she said.

I grabbed a towel off the counter and began cleaning up the mess under her chair. She grabbed the wine bottle and poured herself another in a coffee mug.

"It's all right if you drink," I said. "I'll get you home."

"Sure. Hell you always have. Got me home. He *will* get you home no matter what. He'll bang your lights out till you can't see nothin' but the stars in the sky, but he will by God get you home on time. He will turn into that fantastic dog that saved his dumb butt, like that dumbass prince that sniffed Cindy's shoe. He's so good he knows he just isn't good enough for you. Well up yours prince!"

I was up on one knee, getting up. She meant to just throw the drink in my face, but we were so close the heavy rim of the mug hit my forehead and wine spilled in my hair. Then she punched me on the arm that was in a sling.

"Ouch."

The next thing we were holding each other tight. Just holding on with my hand on the side of her head. I rubbed her hair into my cheek, inhaling her scent. She told me she wasn't leaving and I told her it was OK. She said she meant it this time. Just like before but this time was it. There had been enough damn time and this was it. I told her she'd usually been right about things if unrealistic. She hit me in the arm again.

"Pain never felt so good," I managed. "And I love the taste of wine in your hair."

"Want some more?"

"I'd prefer not to get hit anymore. Look, today made me see some things. We can go to Minaqua in the morning and get the J-P up if you want."

She grabbed a dish towel off the counter and plopped it on my head, then slid slim, strong arms around my neck and told me she didn't care if we could get the J-P up or not.

"I'm not sure what will happen. Your dad and stuff."

"Don't start. I'm eighteen. That part is over. The difference is narrowing. You're now way less than twice my age."

"We can't do anything tonight though," I said. "I've been cut with a dirty knife and had a tetanus shot. I don't know the effects."

She grinned, our mouths inches apart. "Your serious."

"And seriously happy. I think." Her smile faded and one eye narrowed down. "I think I'm really sure," I added.

"Of what?"

I took a breath, expelled it. "You're it, you know that." I kissed her forehead. "You know my thoughts, you're inside my soul. We'll let the world know. But there will be hell to pay for a while."

"Then we'll pay it. I'll rub their noses in the shock of it all."

Ronnie had a way of cutting right to the quick. I always liked that about her. She was going to be my lifetime nose gunner.

We settled into the big comfy chair in front of the window and began talking. Talked the way we always could talk about anything. So close you could feel the other's breath move their body when they talked. We didn't make specific plans, but thoughts zinged in. There was Bonnie being alone. Could we stay in the cabin whenever I was here, starting tonight and going on forever?

"What about Bonnie tonight?" I blurted. "She'll be alone over there."

"I invited Jeanie over to spend the night. Bonnie's good with this. We're covered. You think you're marrying a dummy?"

I grinned with her forehead against my chin.

OK, could we just live at my place in Wausau? Why not? My family would adjust, they loved Ronnie, but what about her parents? Her dad traveled so much we never got to know each other very well. Not well enough so I could just hunker down *vis-a vis* and have a heart to heart about his oldest daughter; 'You see, Paul, we've been lovers since she turned seventeen and discussed it for two years before that, which represented the period when we passed out of the buddy stage and could hardly keep our hands off each other. You know those nature walks we used to take? Well let me tell you, Paul . . . '

I decided the exact truth would not be appropriate in this situation. Perhaps I could couch it in an epiphany . . .

"Quit fretting," she said. "Burton's laughing."

"Why would you say such a thing?"

"He's here right now and he's laughing." She snuggled in against my chest. "I used to talk to him about us. He told me lots about you. The last year and a half before he died."

"Please say you're kidding. You didn't really tell him."

"Sure. Pretty much everything. Even more than I told Bonnie. He was the one person I could talk to about it. I guess it embarrassed him some, but what are friends for?"

"Ronnie. If he would have said anything I'd have gone to prison."

"Don't be silly, Burton knew stuff about most of the people around this lake that would get them jail time. Some he didn't even like, but he never said a bad word about anybody. He was the least judgmental and one of the kindest people I've ever known."

I sighed, tried not to think about the past, the bad thoughts, the names I called myself.

"Once he told me you were the closest thing to a son he'd ever have."

"I sure miss him tonight."

"He's here," she said. "All you have to do is let him in. Listen to the spirits, city boy."

"He loved this country," I said. "And everything in it."

I had a sip of her wine and relaxed some more. I loved it here too, but with Burton and Ronnie it was different, they were elemental to the country. I suppose that was part of the mix in what I felt for Ronnie. The time six months ago when she had arranged a visit with a friend in Green Bay I'd met her there and we had a great time. I bought her presents and took her and her girlfriend to the movies. After I took her friend home the two of us walked along the lake and talked about our imagined future. I rented a room on the sixth floor of a marginal hotel where guests were accorded discreet disinterest. We lit candles in the room and pretended we were in a castle tower and the evil sheriff was hunting us. She loved our games and the city but never once said she wanted to live there.

Later after I'd banked the fire in the stove we pulled a quilt around our shoulders, helping the other get that quilt up around our neck and head until we were shoving it in each other's face, which was funny, and with our heads together looking out the window at the light of the moon on the lake.

Our lake. Our place. It was one of those sharp, very clear nights when you could see beyond the stars.

REPARATION AND THE FRIENDLY NIGHT

Soggy 4 am light, another bumpy ride to work. The beginning of the project and our mother ship hadn't arrived yet so we had to bang our way from Valdez to the job every morning.

Merle's worn, whiskered face jutted into glacial raindrops peppering our faces as the barge plowed and pounded its way to our assigned beach. He stood a little away from the rest, a not very tall man, shapeless under the poncho and sou'wester. We were a mixed lot of laborers, fishermen, college students, bulky in rain gear, here to make a buck on the Exxon-Valdez oil spill. Dirty, hard work when the equipment was running, more tedious when it broke down. No one seemed to know what the hell they were doing or who was in charge. You can have all the steam-heated hot water and high pressure lines you can drag up the rocks, extending like tentacles from vessels scattered like random leaves on a pond as far as you could see along the steep edges and bays of Prince William Sound, but how do you clean a whole beach? You're looking down miles of rocky shoreline saturated with thick, sticky crude and nobody with any experience in coping with such a mess. There never was a spill like this. Dead and dying birds everywhere, sea otter bodies draped over rocks and floating with other carcasses on the oily sea, eagles and seals locked together in black lumps of suffocation. You try to ignore it, the terrible waste of life. It wasn't your fault, you just showed up for the money. Nothing to be done now except the assigned work and occasionally telling one of the reporters full of fake concern to fuck off. The foreman acts like he's pissed when you pop off like that to a leach (what we call anyone in the media), but they aren't really upset, except maybe because in their position they can't say the same.

His stick matches were wet so I stepped forward with my Zippo. Merle looked up sharply from under the brim of his sou'wester, bloodshot eyes narrowed, appraising. He nodded slightly and cupped rough hands around the lighter, drew deeply on the cigarette. His breath smelled of stale liquor and greasy Valdez breakfast. He offered me the pack.

"No thanks. Quit six months ago. I'm Chris." I extended my hand.

"Merle." He seemed vaguely amused as we shook hands. "Why'd you quit?"

"Takes your breath."

Merle nodded, still appraising. "Guess if this tin can tips over then I'll grab onto you. With all that extra wind you should be able to get us both to shore."

I came to understand this was Merle being friendly. He was surprisingly strong, hunkered, his face an old square-toed boot with burning dark eyes that stared right through you. I don't know why he decided to talk to me, or why I was drawn to him. When the equipment broke down they often sent for Merle. He'd usually get the boiler working right or the pump going again. As reward they would let him sit up on the bow of the barge and get drunk. He was oblivious to the low flying planes and news cameras. He'd yell at me on the beach where I'd be staggering around under the weight of the hard thrashing hose, trying to avoid a face full of hot water and sludge. I'd give him the universal gesture and he'd laugh and wave, tip the pint to his mouth with a greasy pinky extended, a touch of finesse that fit his ironic aura. Merle drank enough to be a real Alaskan, although he was from Montana.

"They say you slow down as you get older," Merle told me one evening as we sat at the end of the dock after a long day of blasting the beach. "But I drink more now. Experience, kid. If it goes against you, you drink more or die."

"Drink more and die sooner."

Merle chuckled hoarsely. "So what? Dieing is easy. It's livin' that's complicated. At least for this old dummy. I figure when you're looking at the down slope it don't matter all that much. Long as you have your close people reasonably covered it don't matter."

"But you're a mechanic," I said. "You could be top dog on one of these boats. Or a trouble-shooter up on the line. You don't have to be out here bucking hose with the rest of us."

Merle got that amused look, offered me his pint, a backup after he'd emptied his daily flask. I took a hit, just so he wouldn't get impatient with me. I was learning from him, though I couldn't tell you what exactly.

"I'm no mechanic," he said. "I can just fix machinery. It's part touch and part from necessity. Started on Dad's old tractor. Had to keep it going. Then I learned about cars and diesel trucks. Then one winter I worked on a rock crusher and got into gears and pulleys and the run of a belt. But that ain't what I'm best at."

When he offered I had another sip. Merle was gazing off across the water. A gull screamed overhead and way off I watched an eagle bank into a turn. At that distance I couldn't make out any oil stains, but all the birds around the Sound had them.

It was as if Merle had forgotten I was there. I realized he wasn't waiting for me to ask, so finally I did. "So?"

"Um?" Merle reluctantly pulled his attention back to his immediate surroundings. "What?"

"What you're good at. You said it wasn't mechanics."

"Didn't say I wasn't good at mechanics. Said it wasn't what I'm best at."

I waited, but Merle didn't say anything, just had another pull on the pint. He could be an irritating sonofabitch.

"You going to say, or do I just leave you sitting here to talk to the damn gulls?"

Merle smiled enough to show stained teeth. "I'm a dog man. I'm a very good trainer of dogs."

"Is that your trade?"

"Well, yes it is," Merle said. "Or not. I don't do it to make a living. But I charge for it certainly. I guess you'd call it a avocation. Was anyway. Haven't trained any dogs for two years. Two years and a half. Since Buster died." He looked at the pint, slipped it into an inner coat pocket.

"Had my own way of going about it," Merle continued, voice warming. "Didn't have a regular kennel or anything. Wouldn't take on more than two dogs at a time, maximum. My ranch is the perfect place to train a dog, being surround-ed by good bird and game country, scattered stock, although I didn't go in for training stock dogs. Did train two. Good little dogs, 'specially the border collie. Also trained two dogs for security. But mainly I trained dogs for hunting."

It was the most animated I'd seen Merle, so after a minute or two when he'd stopped talking I pressed him about his experience as a dog trainer.

"What I'd do, see, is listen to a person's needs regarding a dog, and if they seemed all right, the way they talked about the dog and how they might treat it, then I'd take their money. Three thousand or more, depending. They knew it would be up to a year before they could take their dream dog home. I would then have to go and find a puppy. I'd put the word out and people would start calling me." Merle pulled the pint back out and had a quick sip, continued. "So I'd go around looking at puppies until I found the right one. I'd give the people a few dollars and take that puppy home."

"How would you know which puppy was the right one?"

Merle glared at me. "How do you know a frog has a watertight ass? If you have to ask don't mess with it! Go be a doctor or something."

I nodded, declined when he offered the bottle.

"We'll have to get another one soon," Merle said. "And you're buying. Better go now, before we have to pay bar prices."

We walked over to the Trading Post where I bought two pints, a shape that fit the inside pocket of his coat, then retraced our steps to the bench near the pier where our barge was tied up. It was nearly the long summer twilight, a calming time for me. I had lately come to welcome darkness as a mourner welcomes the sanctuary of their shawl.

"Pretty country," Merle said, admiring the shadowed, mountainous terrain where snow still covered most of the high rocky crags, a gleam off the calm, corrupted Sound.

"Not better'n my home country, but nice and rugged

where wild things roam. If I'd a come here when I was young and adventuresome I may have stayed for a time."

"The winters are long and dark. It's pretty depressing." It occurred to me I always said something like this to people who might be thinking about moving to Alaska, just to discourage them. Yet we were only having idle conversation.

"Hell, I know about winter," Merle said. "My ranch is nearly four thousand feet. On the east slope of the Rockies. Some people higher than me can't get their rigs out for weeks. But it ain't so bad. We take care of each other." He spit a powerful wad down on the rocks of the bulkhead. "My wife makes do with what we raise and what I hunt. We eat well all winter."

"What about these puppies you brought home?" I asked. "What did you do with them?"

Merle's leathery face softened. "Well, first off, you just have to let 'em be puppy. Start the basic manners training. Ease into it and watch them for a time. There's no hard and fast recipe, contrary to what some say. They're all different. Each one has their little ways that makes 'em stand out. With a purebred you have tendencies you expect that generally show up right away, imprints of the breed, but that's only the start of it. Setters and Labs are easy usually. Shorthairs can be a little more complicated. Shepherds are the smartest, sometimes easy, sometimes not. My favorite is a part German shepherd and part hunting breed. They mix well with Lab most of the time. That's what Buster was, pure German shepherd and pure yellow Lab, first generation. Best hunting dog there ever was. Birds or ducks, perfect on both. He'd even hunt a rabbit if you asked him to. He helped me train six dogs, and they were all the better for it. That was back before ... well, before the incident."

"Incident?"

Merle's expression darkened, then he turned away and started to get up. He looked around carefully, as if regaining his bearings. "Better get something to eat while there's still slop in the pot. Looks like the line's shortened over at Rosy's."

As we walked toward Rosy's Cafe I told Merle about the dog I had lost recently. "We used to hunt ptarmigan together. He was Lab and pit bull."

"Staffordshire terrier," Merle corrected. "Bull terrier actually. Pit bull came from the neanderthals that fight them in pits or closed rings. It still goes on. It was those dog's bad luck to be good at it."

We dodged a car weaving down the street. "Have you seen a dog fight?"

"Yeah, I seen a few," Merle said tightly. "Back when I was young and stupider. I've seen a Staffordshire fight. They fight low and dirty, being squat dogs and not very heavy. But they have a instinct. They use what they have, which is lots of low end torque and a close-in quickness and powerful jaws. They try to crush the feet of their opponent and then go for the throat when they have the advantage. The automatic love they have for their masters is what makes them such deadly fighters. You know, they don't want to fail a command. It's too bad, because they're nice little dogs by nature." Merle nodded, spit to the side.

"I trained two of them," he continued. "One was mixed and the other purebred. I made them security dogs, but they weren't born killers. You can always tell. They'd do it of course, kill, if they had to. If they get it in their head their parent wants them to. Their owner. But the ones I had were nice little dogs."

We took a booth in Rosy's and Merle ordered the special, meatloaf. I played it safe with a hamburger. "I think a neighbor poisoned Juno," I said.

Merle looked sharply at me. "What are you saying?"

"I'm certain that's what happened to my dog Juno. My neighbor killed him. He thought Juno had killed his cat, but he didn't. A mink killed his cat. I live near a stream."

Merle's jaw line stood out like a drawn bowstring. For the first time I realized his eyes were not brown but mainly black, like the sea during a storm.

"And what did you do?" he demanded.

In that moment I knew my actions had been inadequate. I hadn't taken any action really, because I couldn't prove anything and wasn't sure what I could have done. I told Merle how Juno had crawled up on the back porch and I found him there in great pain when I came home from work. I rushed him to the vet, but it was too late. All the symptoms of poison, the vet said. I took Juno home and buried him in the back yard next to my mother's favorite flowers. The next day I confronted the neighbor and asked him straight out if he knew anything about Juno's death. He pretended surprise, denied knowing anything. But I saw and heard the falseness.

"The thing about a sneak sonofabitch like that," Merle said, "is that if you don't blister their ass they're likely do the same thing again. They have to learn about reparation. One way or another."

Merle was quiet the rest of the time we spent together that evening, stoic, thinking about things he didn't want to share.

The next morning we bucked into a sharp wind on the way to our section of beach and the new guy started puking before we cleared the harbor. Merle didn't jive him like he usually would. He stood well forward, not talking to me or anybody else, taking the spray and thinking his own thoughts. Several crew engaged me, including the girl on board. I was a comparatively seasoned beach cleaner by then and easier to talk to then some of the others. Talking came easy for me. Decisive action was more complicated. Juno had been killed and I felt guilty again. Merle had brought back all those feelings.

Two days later we were in the Flip Flop Saloon after a very nasty, rainy day of blasting the beach and the girl in a fringed bikini they had imported to dance had done her job and the fight down near the entrance had been broken up. We were exhausted, but not the good tired after a hard day, it was one of those almost-full-moon nights when you have a couple more than you need and you can't think of any good reason why.

Merle suddenly turned to me and said, "I know what it's like to lose a good dog to a no-good neighbor. The night Buster was murdered I cried like a baby. I did. While I was buryin' him and after. I couldn't hardly stop. For a time I was not sure I was going to regain control over myself. It was a grief beyond anything I'd known. Worse than when I buried my mother."

We had been drinking about two hours, bar bourbon and beer chasers, tasters Merle called the bourbon. Most of the people in there didn't care squat about the damage that had been done, but they liked the hell out of damage control, which was the source of our fat paychecks. Whether you were from Alaska or Montana or California, Exxon damage control was going to get you through the winter. But it was the kind of improvisational work that made people quirky and dopey-drunk too quickly. A guy from a trawler stood up at the bar and announced that bottom nets like his did more damage in one day than the Exxon-Valdez could ever do and about half the people in there laughed in a way that wasn't funny. Then another fight broke out three stools down, fists flew, glass shattered. Merle and I grabbed our glasses and moved to a wet table that had just been vacated.

"Buster must have been a great dog," I said.

"Yeah." Merle offered me a pack of cigarettes, nodded when I declined, stuck one in his mouth, searched for a match until I fired it with the Zippo I continued to carry in case I met a girl that smoked.

"That's what they call a cliche'," Merle said. "Great dog. There's lots of great dogs. It is the nature of a dog to be great in our eyes. A dog is born to please a human, whether or not they deserve it. With Buster, now, you had a dog that was unusually intuitive – you know that word, intuitive?"

"Yeah, but I never expected you to use it."

Merle chuckled, coughed out smoke in staccato little circles. "I like you, kid," he said. "Eventually I may understand why, considering the problems you wear on your sleeve you won't own up to. Anyway, Buster was unusual in that he learned a thing very fast and permanent. By that I mean you show him and explain something once and he knew it. Once he learned a thing, even something complex like taking a point on a pheasant or marking a shot duck, he'd do it perfect the next time. Even if a chunk of time had passed. I'm saying this in the perfect sense here, not just talking words."

Merle drew long on the cigarette, started the smoke streaming out of his nose and continued, "Buster retained everything I taught him. He was a prince among dogs. Except he couldn't stand me drunk. Wouldn't come near me when I came home drunk, just sat back and stared. Like a parent, dammit. He'd go get the wife up. Bark or whatever until she got up and gave me some hell. But how could I fault him for that? He herded my stock. I've only got about 20 head. Meat for us and a messed up neighbor and to pay the yearly ranch expenses. And if I interrupted him to flush a bird or trail a rabbit, he'd do that and come right back to the other task without missing a beat. Buster actually made me lazy. And he knew it. And he'd coax me into holding up my end. It was the darnedest thing."

I watched Merle take a sip of his beer. He wasn't trying to kid me, this was serious.

"I never had a dog like that," I said. "Juno and I were close, but I can't say he was brilliant in the way you're talking about. We talked, but we didn't have extended conversations in any abstract sense."

Merle snorted smoke, shook his head. I considered the soot-filled creases in his bristly face and the slashing sneer of his hard mouth, wondered when the last time a woman had kissed that mouth passionately. I wondered if he thought about it. Our accommodations of sleeping rooms and a primitive shared bathroom made it difficult to bathe more than twice a week; consternation for me after a hard day's work, no problem for Merle. He was not a seaman even to the degree I was, which wasn't very advanced, yet no one enjoyed the barge trips in and out to the job as much as Merle. He was a throwback, fearless in a way most people do not wish to challenge. To me he seemed to possess an intrinsic knowledge to survive in any wilderness.

"The abstract in your terms means nothing to a dog," Merle said. "A dog dreams his own abstractions. They experience their own abstractions. They know you won't get theirs, why would you expect them to understand yours?"

"That makes too much sense," I said. "At least for this senseless day."

I got out of there and spent the night dreaming about Juno. In the dream I sent neighbor Newberg down Ship Creek on an air mattress and watched him disappear into the swirling silt rips of Cook Inlet. He screamed at the end, his twisted mouth wide open as he was sucked down into the tumbling milky water. I turned and smiled at Juno who leaned his tawny head toward my shoulder the way he would when we were high up on a ridge listening to ptarmigan calling in the valley below. Juno may have been a bull moose in the house but in the high country he was a ballet. He swam like an otter and probably would have preferred to hunt waterfowl, but I liked the high country and hunting ptarmigan so he learned how to scent, stalk and point. He was a big, powerful dog with blunt features, yet when he hunted those fast-flushing birds he was beautiful grace. Well above the trees which stopped at less than 2,000 feet, where the wild flowers last only weeks, Juno and I would stalk the birds so many other animals up there stalked and I would get this sense that we were a legitimate part of the landscape.

The next morning was a nice ride out on the barge, not raining, some blue sky showing. With the good weather the planes and cameras were around. The skipper told us in a few days a ship would be anchored off our site and we wouldn't have to run in and out every day, just tie up to the ship like the other cleaners were doing, like puppies suckling their mother. We had just got going well on a stretch of beach when there was a sharp crack from the barge and the hose went limp. No water out of Merle's hose either. They yelled from the barge and said an adapter housing had shattered. A new one was already on its way. Down about one-point-five hours.

We straightened our hoses to the barge's drift and pulled off our raincoats just as the sun came out bright and warm.

"Let's take that dry rock up there," Merle suggested.

It was a great vantage point to watch the other boats and workers up and down the shoreline until we lost sight of them around another indentation.

"Strange way to make a livin'," Merle observed, after taking a nip from the stainless steel flask he refilled every night. He offered it to me and I declined.

"People been raping this old earth for a long time without much care," Merle continued. "Now they're payin' us top wages to clean up a mess we can't really clean very well. Shooting our hot water on these old rocks. Nature will have to clean it properly. All those cameras and planes and politicians hovering around are just fluff. Like our efforts today. Sitting here and waiting for a part that may or may not come. It doesn't really matter. We don't matter here."

"Your opinion about this situation doesn't matter much this morning," I said.

"Hell, I know that. Doesn't matter much any morning. So what's eating you?"

"Nothing."

Merle laughed coarsely. "You're like a open book, kid, 'cept the damn words are all mixed up. You can tell ol' Merle. Ain't nobody else gonna ever know."

"You're already drunk. They get that part on and you won't be able to handle your hose."

"Be mid-afternoon by the time they get that part on and the boiler fired again. By then I'll be sober and ready for some overtime. Might as well say what you want to say."

"Had a dream about my dog last night," I said quick, just trying to get it out so he'd shut up. "It was a nice dream. I killed my neighbor. It was fine in the dream but it doesn't set so well now, maybe because I didn't feel any remorse."

Merle nodded, took another sip.

"That stuff will kill you quick if you start using it in the morning," I said.

"I know it," Merle replied. "But it holds down Rosy's meatloaf. One excuse's good as another. Maybe you shouldn't feel remorse, kid. I don't."

"Yeah, well, what else are you going to say? You're still mourning your perfect dog. What the hell did *you* do anyway? Besides blame some neighbor. Maybe he didn't even do it."

Merle took more than a sip, grimaced as it hit the back of his throat. He put the flask away. "Oh, he did it all right. He did a number of things."

"Such as?" I challenged.

Merle didn't even look my way, just started talking.

"We had a common road almost to the highway and the fool ran over several of my chickens because he never watched where he was going. Funny about that common road. I never wanted it but there was a easement written into my bill of sale regarding the adjoining property, and fate brought me that dumb sonofabitch. He set coyote traps on my land and caught one of my newborn calves. Number four jump trap, big enough for a wolf, which he thought had invaded us. Set that trap on my land and caught my calf when it was a few days old. Broke its leg. The mother's bawling brought in coyotes and they did bad things to that calf before I got there to run 'em off.

"He was always shooting at some damn thing. Bullets flyin' around like we were in a war zone. Gut-shot a spike muley while it was drinking out of the creek and it came running right through my yard, put a hoof through one of my little greenhouses. I had to put that deer out of its misery in the middle of our vegetable garden. Then he got a used dirt machine, made in Asia, had a trail blade for it. Started gouging trenches everywhere. Managed to mess up the little creek that ran between our land with his infernal excavations. Then one night he killed the best dog in the state."

There was no tolerance in Merle's face now. No mercy. For a moment I thought about leaving him there high on the beach and trying to wave in the skiff.

"Why would he kill Buster?" I asked finally.

"Because he was stupid. Had no sense about anything. No, not stupid, that's not fair to stupid people with good intentions. Twisted moron fits better. Thought we'd been invaded by wolves for God's sake. Wolves coming down from Canada to get his few measly sheep. As if Mr. Wolf cared about him or his sheep."

There was a few seconds of silence, then I said, "So there were wolves around?"

"Oh, we usually get a few in the winter from up north. I'd see two or three now and then, setting just inside the trees, watching. But they never did much harm. More good than harm. They take out some sick elk and deer. Several small herds spend most of the winter down the valley a ways. When he's in the neighborhood, Mr. Wolf also takes out a few coyotes, which we have more than enough of. They will make a bloody mess of a coyote. But they never bothered the idiot's sheep. I'm sure enough of that."

"So what happened?" It was one of those questions you feel compelled to ask even though you don't really want to take it any further.

Merle adjusted himself on the rock, spit to one side. "Clear night. Crisp. Full moon and a easy north wind. Nice pale light and a dusting of snow so you could see things moving. Let Buster out to make his late rounds, make sure everything was all right. My wife went to bed and I thought I heard something, then nodded off while I was reading. Next thing I know there's a knock on the door. Sheriff came in. We knew each other. Told me there had been a accident.

Sheriff repeated that, 'There has been a accident.'"

Merle reached into his jacket for the flask, but his hand came out empty. It had been an automatic reaction he rejected.

"Sheriff said my neighbor Joe thought he saw a wolf," Merle, continued. "So he fired a shot. Except it wasn't a wolf. It was Buster. I can recall the sound of the clock over by the hallway ticking and we stood like that for maybe a minute. Finally I asked him where this took place, and the sheriff tells me down by the creek. And I asks him where by the creek. And he says that Joe was on his side of the creek and Buster was on his own side, but Joe saw this silhouette and thought it was a wolf. So I asks him, You mean Buster was on his own land, up on the bank of the creek, and Joe shot him. And he says that was apparently what happened, but it was a accident and Joe's real sorry. Real sorry, he says again. Joe said he wants to pay something towards another dog."

Merle slowly shook his head and I saw muscles ripple along his black-whiskered jaw.

"Eventually I just says accidents happen. And then I tells the sheriff I have to go take care of Buster. He had the guts to warn me then, so I told him to get the hell out. Then I went down by the creek and found Buster. And I took him to his favorite place next to the back porch where the ground was kind of hard and cool. And I buried him. I got the pick out of the shed and broke into that hard ground and dug down deep. My wife sat on the porch steps watching me. When I was done she brought me a drink without a word. Then I told her to go on to bed, I'd stay up for a while."

Merle just stared off at nothing in particular. At everything in particular.

"Handling it like that," I said. "You were cooler than I probably would have been."

"Yeah," Merle said. "I was pretty cool. Accidents happen, like I told the sheriff. But he was waiting for me at the Y later. I was on my way to Joe's with my 12 gauge loaded with buck. That sheriff knew me pretty well. Had his patrol car across the road. Couldn't get by. I cursed him, said I'd shoot him too. But he was the cool one, talked me down. That's when I knew I would have to take care of the matter in another way."

A cool wind had started with the sunshine and now blew steadily out of the northwest. The water turned a milky blue-green. Down the way two eagles screamed and tore at each other over a carcass. It was too far to make out what the dead had been.

"You buy a piece of land," Merle continued. "You just want to live your own way, pay your own way, let others do the same. You help neighbors in the ways that you can. You build something, become part of a community. Then some destructive loony comes in and ruins it. No logical reason. Like a mad dog in your yard."

"Look, Merle, you don't have to give me all – "

He suddenly turned and glared. "Shutup and *listen.* You're not accountable and I don't have to worry about you talkin'. You like to talk, kid, but you don't say much. That's your integrity. You talk but you don't tell. And because of your own dog you won't tell this. But you'll feel better for knowing it."

"No," I said, looking out at the water. "I don't want to know what you did."

"*The hell you don't.* You're dying to know. And when you do you'll rest easier."

I shook my head, refusing to look at him.

"I started on his well," Merle said quietly. "That's how I started. Dumped sheep shit down there until he got sick.

Him and his mangy hound. Felt a little sorry for the hound. Then I went out at night and stuck several of his sheep with a sharp stick dipped in their own shit. Covered the hole with wax. Those sheep got a peritonitis infection and started swellin' up and diein' off. Out there in the sage like piles of wool with feet sticking up in the air. And he didn't have a clue about the why of any of it. He just got crazier. I sat up there above the creek and watched it happen."

"I said I don't need to know –"

"*Shutup.*" Merle took a long pull from the flask then and got a look on his face I couldn't look at for long. It was a look so stark you didn't want to hear what was coming.

"Joe started plowing up his yard," Merle continued in a voice as cold and sharp as a razor. "Plowed the hell out of it one day clear down to the little bluff with that Asian dozer. So that night I go over there and crawl under his machine. It's on a slope right above the drop into the creek. No way to leave a piece of equipment. All the oil and fuel draining away from where it should be. I got this little pencil light in my mouth and I do some things to his clutch linkage. Never figured it for any final thing, but the next morning he comes out and starts the machine. Smoke puffs out of the stack and he stuffs the gear lever and it gets away from him right away. Starts rolling backwards. I'm sitting on the bank above the creek, almost at the exact spot where he killed Buster, and I see him looking around frantic as his machine starts rolling backwards. And I see how it's going to be. The machine goes over backward with him still jerking his head around and pulling levers and crashes down end over end into the creek. Just before it hits bottom he gets thrown out and the machine lands on him.

"I'm sitting there watching this. I sit there for a couple of minutes, maybe longer, maybe a half hour, looking at

that Asian machine half buried in the creek. Water eddy-
ing around the cowl. Smoke drifting up lazy-like out of the
engine compartment.

"Then I go in the house and call the sheriff. And I say,
'Sheriff, there's been a accident.'"

After a long silence, Merle said, "Fast boat headed our
way. We may have to do a little work today yet. C'mon, kid,
the tide's taking our lines."

That night I went off alone and drank too much and met
an attractive girl who I could have gone home with and
didn't. She had a lot of baggage too; it didn't mesh with mine,
but I was thankful for her company. Not long before I would
have gone with her anyway, the hell with baggage, I could always think about woulda-coulda-maybe-I-shouldn't-a in the
morning, or forget the whole thing and just go to work. But
Merle had reminded me of things I'd avoided thinking about,
a vision of myself at a younger time when Diana had decided
we were not going to get married because she'd met another
poet. They were two poets in love. Right after that I began
losing track of who I'd thought I was and felt a disconnect,
adrift and belonging nowhere and to no one. Even my family
and friends would appear ghost-like, drifting at the edges of
my awareness and efforts to connect would not bring them
closer and I realized I didn't mind that much that they were
not closer. Diana and I had started dating in high school. We
were friends before we were lovers. I'd thought that part
of my life was set. Then Juno died. After that I would imagine seeing pieces of myself in trash strewn along the road.
I was looking at thirty in a couple years, living in my parent's basement, money in the bank, little piece of property
in the Chugach foothills and no prospects. Footloose and
unencumbered. No burning desire except to go somewhere
where I might find some oxygen to feed the flame burning

up my insides.

Later I dreamed about Juno again and sent Newberg down Ship Creek on an air mattress again, but it wasn't so bad this time. It was more vivid than the first time but not unpleasant because although I hadn't done to Newberg what he had done to Juno, I thought I could now. I wanted Newberg to see this in me and couldn't wait to get home. I wanted to meet his eyes and wave to him on his way to his T-Bird in the morning. I wanted to get into his dreams. This attitude did great things for my own dream experiences. Juno and I got together every night for a long time after that, sometimes to hunt the high country, sometimes to just say hello and pal around. He had other things going on too, things beyond my understanding, like mine must have been to him. But it's very pleasant whenever we get together.

I heard Merle quit the cleanup the week after I did.

Some months later I got a half page scrawled letter and a photo from him. In the picture he's holding a black and white puppy. The puppy's eyes are very bright and Merle is almost smiling. I still don't know what to make of him, this man who appeared in my life and made me see and feel certain things in a new way. I know I'm not like him, but I don't mean that in any negative way. He was on my side for reasons he understood better than me, and if I'm ever in Montana I'll look him up.

Thinking about this reminded me of a friend of mine down on the Kenai who had a Golden Lab that was expecting. Those pups would be about a month, month-and-a-half old now. I did owe him a visit.

SMOKEY

It seems now like unrelated events in my life were connecting to achieve some logical design, like a paint-by-number mosaic, except at the time I could not see the picture emerging, which I'm now sure was just as well.

I was dating a guy named Steve who had a beautiful Siberian husky named Ursa. She was a very nice dog, but when I realized I was beginning to like Ursa more than Steve, who had a drinking problem, it seemed like the time had come to go our separate ways. It wasn't that Steve didn't have reason to continue torturing himself with booze, he carried some serious emotional scars and I could sympathize with his experiences and motives, but I didn't want to live inside his problems for the rest of my life. When I found the empty mini-bottles behind the seat in his truck I realized he was hitting the booze on his way from work and probably during the day and I couldn't deal with it any longer.

Just before we ended our stormy relationship Ursa mated with a German shepherd. This event unfolded in Steve's front yard. All parties present seemed satisfied and Steve thought the mix of breeds a good one.

Shortly thereafter Steve and I parted, although I agreed to keep in touch. Determined to reassert my priorities I moved to a different residence across town, half of a duplex on the outskirts of Salt Lake City. It was simple and cozy with blooming lilacs and a tall willow tree out the living room window, a nice enough place for my main endeavor, which was continuing to develop my skill and style as an impressionist painter, a process that takes many years, though in the beginning you think you can beat the clock on development. I couldn't, but once you get in the hunger keeps growing and you can't let it go. I soon settled into working a regular job and painting whenever I could. One day, as I was working on a new canvas, I looked out the window and saw Steve's pickup pull up in front of my gate. My first thought was, Oh no, what now.

Steve ambled in that slow way he moved after he'd done something stupid, a sort of low, sneaky gait up to the front door, carrying a shoebox out in front of him. I opened the door enough to ask what he wanted. Steve removed the lid from the shoebox. Inside were three newborn, blind puppies, two gold-colored males and a black female. They had damp, thick coats and squeaked in unison as they cuddled together, burrowing their blunt little muzzles into each other. My first impulse was to cuddle them, but I held back.

"They're just two days old," Steve said. "Ursa died giving birth. The vet said it was probably liver failure. Guess there's some irony to that."

I shut my eyes and wondered what had happened to that poor dog. How could Ursa's liver have failed? Then I realized it wasn't fair to presume. Steve would never mistreat an animal.

"The vet told me I'd have to raise these pups with a bottle and give them formula and stuff," Steve said. "But you know, my track record with bottles isn't very good. I want to take care of them, but it just won't work out. And I don't want something bad to happen to these pups. I don't know where else to take them. Please, Debra, you have to do it."

I put my hands to the sides of my head, covering my ears, but his words were already in there. "Are you crazy? You know my schedule. I already have a cat. How can I possibly do this?"

"I know," Steve said, setting the box down on the porch. "And I'm sorry. But there isn't anyone else. You're the only one who can do it. I know you'll find a way. If you can just get them through the first few weeks, I'll find homes for them. All of them. I promise."

I looked down at the puppies squeaking in the box, trying to find their mother.

"Just a few weeks," Steve repeated. "I already know someone that will probably take a pup."

Trapped, I thought, like a butterfly with a pin through my heart. If I refused Animal Control would no doubt eliminate these helpless puppies immediately. Well, a few weeks didn't sound too extreme. For a few weeks I could do anything. Maybe the experience would give my painting some new insight. I looked up to see Steve hurrying down the walk.

I took the shoebox of squirming bodies to the pet store and loaded up on real young puppy food and relevant paraphernalia. There were choices to make and I didn't have a clue, so I just bought. But over the next few extraordinary days the puppies helped sort it all out. We settled on Esbilac formula and small, disposable, latex nipples. There is also a best angle for the bottle during feeding and a specific squeak tone that means it's feeding time. Feeding time comes often, every two or three hours, not unlike new human babies. Potty time also comes often. Imagine yourself with newborn triplets and you'll get the general idea.

Of course I still had to go to work every day. My only choice was to recruit a shift of workers: a niece, two of my most sympathetic friends, my sister who tried to resist until I handed her a puppy. These women rearranged their lives in order to help. Beyond feeding and keeping them clean, the puppies had to be held. Newborn puppies must be in constant contact with their mother for warmth, reassurance and all the nuances of bonding. I became their mother, with several part-time moms, and we all learned to do things while holding puppies: cleaning the house, reading, personal things. When someone came to visit, they were expected to hold puppies. The tiny dogs were always trying to wag their tails and nurse something; your finger, chest, chin, earring.

The puppies grew very fast. In about a week their eyes popped open and they were ready to rock. It was a big world and they wanted to see it all. It was about this time that Puff, the cat, entered her period of emotional instability. When I came home from work I was greeted with a chorus that sounded like feeding time at a kennel in strained high C. Now when anyone came to visit they did not hold helpless little blind puppies, rather they were descended upon by a small canine hoard greeting them as they would have if their real mother had brought friends home. In fact they did not yet know any other dogs. In the world they knew, humans were parents and I was Mom One. Puff? They had decided she was a live toy, which prompted the cat to insist on spending more and more time outside. Even if it was raining.

Basically puppies took over my life. When I had to go somewhere other than work, the puppies rode along in ever-larger boxes. Their growth process remained on full speed ahead. Soon it was like trying to carry an operating clothes dryer around everywhere you went.

I knew they were weaned the day I heard Puff growling from her safe spot on the counter. I looked where she was glaring and saw the puppies gathered around her food dish, chomping down cat food. The cat became too nervous to turn her back to the room and eat out of her dish. For a brief period Puff thought she'd found a haven on top of a drapery pole. Until her weight caused the pole to come crashing down one afternoon while she was asleep, and the puppies, thinking this was a new game Puff had invented for their amusement, instantly piled on top of her.

Soon after that I had to give poor, stressed-out Puff to my sister, who said the cat wouldn't come out from under the bed. Her food dish had to be slid under there in the dark.

Eating solid food seemed to accelerate the puppies' obnoxious behavior, especially the two gold-colored males. They became a gang of house wreckers, working together to knock down gates and other barricades separating them from somewhere they wanted to go, which was wherever you didn't want them to go. The mostly black female, who I called Smokey, tended to be more conservative, unless her two brothers engaged her in one of their wild games. It was impossible not to like the puppies, but I was new at being a dog mom, and when it came to training I wasn't sure how to proceed with one much less three at a time.

When the puppies were three months old Steve reappeared and said he'd found homes for the two males.

"You told me you were going to find homes for all of them within weeks."

Steve nodded, avoiding my accusing gaze. "I know," he said in his reproachful voice, "and I will. You just have to keep the black one a little longer."

"What kind of people are you giving Buck and Goldfinger to?"

Steve nodded assurance. "They're OK. One has a 12-year-old boy. The other guy I met on the job. He has a nice family." Steve was working his fingers around the edge of his Cat Diesel cap. "But you know, we don't run together or anything. A beer once in awhile, that's it." He looked at me. "These are good homes for the dogs."

I believed him. Some things Steve took seriously.

"All right. I'll keep Smokey for awhile longer."

By the next day I felt like the old lady who lived in a shoe and every kid but one had left. What a relief.

The one that stayed was my secret favorite. Of course Smokey was lonely without her brothers. I made her a cozy new bed and put it next to me during the night. When she would whine from loneliness I would put my hand down to comfort her. She would lick my hand and then cuddle against it, the way she would sleep with her two brothers.

Often I would get up and take her out. I would sit on the porch while she ran around the yard, her nose full of the scent of her litter mates, trying to locate them. She would come close and stare into my face, hoping for an answer to the pain she felt. I would hug her and try to get her into a game, like throw the ball, but for about a week she was lost. What did happen in that week though was that she became housebroken. She made a connection that going outside to potty was a good, fun thing and it soon became her favorite game, toys were secondary. All she had to do was whine during the night and Mom would get up and take her outside and praise her for going potty. Then if she pressed the point mom would play ball. Smokey became expert at tracking balls under dark bushes.

Our bond grew stronger, as it was bound to I guess, now that there were just the two of us. A few nights after the separation I awoke feeling a breath on my face. I remember wondering vaguely why I wasn't afraid, and turned to see Smokey a few inches away. Watching me. No animal had ever looked at me in that way, but in those quiet moments something happened that changed my definition of what an animal is. After that morning I can't really say there was ever any conscious training regimen.

At four months Smokey's demeanor began to noticeably change. Instead of running blindly out into the yard she surveyed it first. On our walks she seemed to automatically accept the leash, it was no longer a restraint, simply the way things should be, and she liked being watchful while walking along at my side. A welcome trait Smokey had inherited from her husky mother was that she seldom barked – always watchful, but quiet. We walked and ran together and made small discoveries in weed patches and often Smokey seemed to read my mind. Teaching her to come, halt and sit, and whatever was so seamless I can't say I ever taught her anything. She just knew what I wanted her to do, and I knew what she needed from me, and that is how it was. There was a growing thing between us so deep it was like the strongest human attachment, but different, because Smokey was not human and I could not be a dog. Yet there was such a mutual desire to close this gap that, while frightening in a way, it was also exciting to me, and natural.

Seven months later Steve came back and said he'd found a home for the female.

"Well, yes," I told him. "She has a home. It is here. With me."

Steve seemed confused. "But I promised her to someone. A nice person."

"I raised this dog on a bottle and we've lived together for ten months. This is her home now."

I wasn't trying to be tough with Steve that night. Not that I would not have been, but I knew there was no way Smokey would have gone with him. We had something beyond Steve's perception and I guess I did not fully understand that until he came to my door that night. It was a visit I still value, because it made everything clear.

The bond between us continued to deepen. Smokey began anticipating things I was about to do before I did them. There was a store nearby where I would walk in the morning for a coke. When I decided to start for the store I would look around and Smokey would already be near the door ready to go. Once I came out of the store and a woman was standing near Smokey. "I've been watching that dog watch you inside the store," the woman said. "She never takes her eyes off you. I don't think I've ever seen such love in an animal's eyes before. You two must be very close."

"Yes," I said, smiling. Smokey was smiling too.

A few weeks later we were walking down a street away from our neighborhood. At seventy pounds Smokey was nearly at her full adult size and her thick, dark coat bounced and shimmered when she walked. She had patches of tan on her underfur, chest and eyebrows and her alert ears were naturally vertical, like her German shepherd father's. Although a leash was unnecessary to keep her at my side, that day it was lucky she was hooked up. At least it was lucky for the man who suddenly stepped out of the alley and blocked our path.

Whatever his intent, Smokey was having none of it. She immediately became a snarling dynamo straining at the leash. It was all I could do to hold her. Her teeth seemed to have grown into giant fangs. The man quickly stepped back into the alley, and just as quickly Smokey calmed. She kept a low growl going until we had passed the alley entrance, and then resumed her cheerful gait as if nothing had happened. It took me a little longer to get over the encounter. There were similar protective instances, yet Smokey never bit anyone. I think her warnings were so convincing that real violence was avoided.

One morning I routinely let Smokey out in the yard and went into the kitchen to put dishes in to soak. There was a sudden crash in the direction of the door. I went to investigate just as Smokey hurled herself against the screen door, then again. She had never done such a thing. I hurried to let her in and looked around the front of the house, wondering what had caused her to act so strangely. Smokey pressed against my legs, obviously trying to convey some urgency. I closed and locked the door and returned to the kitchen with the dog pressing my legs at each step. Something was wrong, but I couldn't figure out what it might be. I touched her head and felt trembling. I began trembling too. Then as I turned to my dishes the whole counter began to shake and the floor moved under me.

It was an earthquake of six plus magnitude.

The thing about an earthquake is that by the time you figure out what is happening and choose a course of action it's usually over. As the tremors receded I realized I was hugging Smokey, and her trembling was receding too. As the last tremor disappeared, Smokey licked my cheek and lay down next to the counter, telling me it was indeed over and I could wash the dishes now.

For sixteen years Smokey couldn't bear to be away from me. When I was painting she would lie nearby and watch every brush stroke. If I went to get a glass of water she would follow without being intrusive. At twelve years of age she became ill and began failing. The vet said her time was very near and I would have to make a decision soon. My husband of several years gently asked how long I was going to let it go on. I could not bear to even consider these questions. I refused to accept what was happening. Some dogs live much longer, I rationalized. And Smokey does not want to leave me.

In retrospect I think Smokey would have accepted passing quietly into that mysterious night, but I could not accept it then. I kept seeing her as a young dog romping in the first winter snow, digging a channel around the yard with her nose, loving the coolness against her thick coat. A tiny blind thing cradled in my arms, suckling the bottle, then I would turn to see her smiling up at me as I was painting. She was my protector and friend and more. She was mixed up inside my spirit in a way that went beyond words and practical questions and all those cold facts about dog years. I could not let her go.

When she became physically unable to get up I would put towels down and, though I wouldn't call myself a particularly strong woman, carry her from room to room. When I turned from a painting she was still there, smiling up at me, and I knew the next stroke and the next color would be better. I was convinced that without her I could not paint, at least not anything anyone would like. Without her the color would fade and the mix would go flat.

Smokey suffered gladly for nearly four more years. I knew she was suffering. Pain pills couldn't block it all. Some days even carrying her caused her great pain. But it was a greater pain for her to be in a different room than I was in. That was a constant with every breath she took. She stayed on and I nursed her. We were still together.

Finally Smokey could hold on no longer. Although I continued to nurse her, the request was now in her eyes. Please let me go. It is time. Please.

When I carried her in the vet was wisely silent and did not try to assist me. The paper crinkled as I laid her down on the table. I held her head and stroked her as he gave her the shot, saw her eyes slowly close and felt her weight relax against me.

They say letting go is always hard. Of course it is. But for me the answer to the obvious question is yes, of course it was. It is still hard sometimes when I look at one of my paintings and see a stroke that reminds me of Smokey. But in those quiet, gentle moments, how could I ever think it wasn't worth it?

DOWN ON THE TRACKS
Summer 1952

"Hobos and winos," my mother said, aiming the little brush she used on her eyebrows at me. "You *better* be careful. Don't get too close, and for *heaven's* sake don't ever go inside their shacks. I know you," she said grimly, "you're gullible even for a thirteen year old."

"Fourteen in seven months."

"Just too curious for your own good. Those people are *desperate.* They can turn violent at the drop of a hat. They've chosen to live outside society, down in the mud and trash with no respect for society's laws."

I nodded to show I was listening. My mother wouldn't steer me wrong on purpose, she just didn't know much about our neighborhood, blaming hobos and winos for everything bad that happened when they usually just wanted to be left alone.

In the morning she took the streetcar to her work downtown. They had lots of parties where she worked so she was often real late getting home. Apparently there's lots of happy-go-lucky people in the insurance business. Not that she wasn't right in saying I was curious and adventurous beyond normal cautionary behavior. This mostly had to do with my hunter instinct and skill in the woods, which were areas I was born to pursue. It was hard when you lived in a city and this wasn't even my home country. Where we had to live now was mainly flat land along the Mississippi River in South St. Louis where it gets so humid and hot in summer it's like breathing underwater. People took sheets and slept in the park, though they'd sometimes get attacked by perverts.

Near midnight, when I'd be waiting for the paper truck I worked on that summer, the big dials over the grocery store would say 90 temperature and 90 humidity. Crazy people were on the night streets, drunks and ravers, mean ones you knew by their dead eyes, kids my age and older up to no good, and the scariest of all – cops: *Get outta here kid or I'll give ya another asshole.* Negroes from the other side of Broadway hung in small groups moving through bands of yellow light and shadows. I hadn't known any up in my home country, but I noticed around here they were not treated the same in the stores and other places I went. Sometimes a Negro I didn't even know would look at me with black hate, although the one's I talked to at the shoeshine stand at Broadway and Jefferson seemed agreeable. They did well at that location shining shoes and I wanted to learn the trade, a way to make money during the winter after school by going in the taverns and giving a shine right there while they were having their beer, and one of those Negro fellas showed me some tricks and told me what kind of brush to buy: *Niggers'l cut you for no reason*, they said. But I never saw this and we all carried knives, you had to be ready for anything.

Now I had to look out for the tracks people where I ran my trap line with Cindy. She's a part husky and part-something-smaller whitish dog I got in the mail from friends of my mother. They named her, I always made that clear. She came named and not very special in appearance, but she became exceptional in her ability to climb steep terrain, which I taught her, and she has a protective instinct she acquired on her own. In pure smarts I guess she's somewhere in the middle of the pack, but we make a pretty good team along the river.

The river here is a big roiling mass you can hardly see light through a glassful, the shoreline muck ugly and polluted. Only scrap fish like carp and gar can live in that water. But along its banks, between the railroad tracks and river, in a narrow strip of bent trees and brown sandy mud that rises to the tracks, flattens for the track bed, then rises sharply up into woods and gullies before the mostly flat land of the city, down there on railroad property the railroad or anybody else doesn't care about, there are small places on the river side of the tracks where people live. Some are just mangy shacks, but others are like small houses with little porches and smoke stacks sticking out of the roofs. From up in the woods above the tracks these places look pretty neat and clean, cozy. On any halfway flat spots around these nicer places are gardens with strings for pea vines, rows of cabbages and carrots and stuff like that growing.

Sometimes Cin and me would just sit up there in the woods watching the people fix things around their tiny houses, root in their gardens, often times just slouch on their porches looking out at the brown river. It seemed like a good way to spend a hot afternoon and I wondered how these people got that way and chose to build their homes here. Behind us the city was a strange and dangerous place, but here we were on

our own without anybody closing in or trying to take something we had. When we'd be down low along the tracks I'd say
hello to one of them sometimes, and they were usually polite
right back.

Then Cindy had that accident. It was mostly my fault, I
should have kept her closer to me along the real steep part
above the little bluff. We'd gone that way plenty of times and
she knew where the trail was. But she was hunting, so in that
sense she counted on me to give her direction. She was on
some scent below me, side-hilling along, and all of a sudden
she just lost traction on the steep ground.

I heard the beginning of her slide as she headed for the
bluff.

"Cin!" I yelled, took a step off the trail and almost fell myself. She went over the edge and dropped about twenty feet
to the tracks.

I came down fast where there was a cut in the bluff, slid
and went into a roll and bounced off a couple little trees,
crashed through some brush and heard a cry, like a woman's
cry, went running for Cin where she was lying over the track,
two paws on each side.

But it wasn't my dog making the sounds.

I started to pick her up. A voice said, "Best to leave her a
minute. Something might be broken."

I looked up as the man put down his sack of groceries. His
dog was nearby, a black and white mop-head dog with stubby
legs and raggy ears, big sad eyes and a wail coming out of it
like I'd never heard any dog make. It was crying for my dog. It
just kept crying and crying while little grunting sounds came
out of Cindy.

"Breath is gone," the man said. He put a large gentle hand
on her back as it rose and fell with Cin's spasms.

"She straddled the tracks you see." He raised his head and

I looked into watery blue eyes soft and sad as a bruise on a baby, and saw nothing bad in there.

"Quite a fall," he said, gazing up at the bluff.

"She never fell before. She can climb anywhere. You think any bones are broke?"

He blinked, slow like so you could watch his eyelids go up and down. "Well . . ." He ran big slow hands over Cin's front legs, slowly through short hair across her back, around my hands, then her ribs, rear haunches, legs, frowned into her glassy eyes, stroked her muzzle.

"I think she's going to be OK," he said. "We have to wait to be sure. Let her catch her breath." He had a nice slow way of talking.

Still his little dog cried. "Why's it doing that?" I asked.

"Oh." He glanced at his dog, went back to stroking Cindy. "She's sensitive to suffering. Some animals are like that."

One of my knees was on the track and I felt a vibration. "Train coming."

"It's a ways off yet," the man said, cocking his head to look into Cindy's ears and eyes. "Let's give her a bit more time, then if you don't mind I'll pick her up and she can rest at my place until the train passes. I have some pain medication if she needs it."

The locomotive came growling around the bend, cars banging along behind. I studied the man, his easy manner, decided he was all right. "She may not let you. I'm the only one picks her up. She weighs almost fifty pounds."

"Maybe if you told her it was OK for me to pick her up?"

"Maybe." I bent down and spoke to Cin the way I did when it was important. The man slid his arms under her chest and stomach. She whimpered a little but let him pick her up. When he had her full weight she made a squeaky noise and he paused, then slowly lifted. He seemed to know what he was doing.

The train was pretty close now, shaking the ground where we stood between the tracks. The man didn't seem in any hurry. This was the fast afternoon train that always pulled over a hundred cars, not like the ones Lenny and I hopped sometimes. We got off the tracks with a little to spare and walked along next to the roaring, clanking train with dust swirling in the flat light and the man carrying my dog to his tiny house. He had one of the nicer houses. It was about twenty feet from the rumbling train and the porch shuddered under our feet.

The porch went around two sides of the house. On the river side were two old kitchen chairs with rusty chrome legs. He put my dog down between these chairs, next to some flowers in a wooden box, and went inside. I put one knee down on the weathered boards of the porch, began stroking Cin and stayed ready just in case. She was breathing a little better. The man came back and poured water out of a pitcher through his fingers and sprinkled it down on Cin's head and neck as she kind of gazed around. The man's little dog started licking water drops off my dog's face.

"She's coming around," the man said. "Might be internal injuries, but they should heal on their own. You might want to take her to a vet to make sure."

"We can't afford any vet just for a checkup." His dog was really beginning to get to me with the whining and licking.

"After your dog gets done she'll probably be healed up anyway."

The man chuckled. Behind me the end of the train passed and the harsh metallic sounds gradually faded. This man seemed nice enough and his clothes were cleaner than mine, a faded U.S. Army shirt, battered military boots. A scar ran down his left cheek and disappeared behind where part of his ear was missing. There was something strange in his face and he was kind of old, forty maybe, with some gray in his whiskers, and he'd limped carrying my dog.

"Jane does get carried away," he said in his slow way. "She's kind of an old sob sister."

"You named your dog Jane?"

The man's face went dark, like a cloud came over. "My wife named her. For her aunt." He brightened a little. "But then her aunt had a cat named Frederick."

"Oh, man . . ." I had to laugh, and then he did too, which you could tell wasn't something he was used to. Then I said, "What about your groceries?" He looked confused, so I jumped up and said, "I'll get 'em. You watch my dog."

Some stuff had spilled out next to the tracks, but no damage done, just catsup and mayo, bread marked with a yellow day-old sticker, chicken wings and jar of pickles. When I got back Cindy was in a half sitting position. I gave the man the sack and got down next to my dog. When I put my arm around her she gave me a lick in the face.

"You get that one free," I told her. "I should have seen you in a bad place down there and called your ass back up to the trail. You didn't find nothin' so don't be taking chances like that anymore."

The man came out of his little house carrying an open bottle of Hires' Root Beer. He offered it to me.

I thought about it, shook my head. "Thanks anyway. I appreciate what you did for my dog, but I can't take anything from you."

He studied the bottle of root beer as if it were something he no longer recognized, then stared out across the river. "I've seen you with your dog up on the bluff," he said quietly. "Sometimes you have a rifle."

"Yeah. I got a Remington twenty-two. It's just a single

shot, but maybe this winter I can buy a pump." I squinted up at him in the afternoon light. "I'm a hunter and trapper when I'm not working or in school. What do you do?"

His lips made an odd smile and he sat down. Slowly his eyes moved up to stare at the sky. The root beer hung from his hand. I thought I better say something.

"Did you build this place?"

He seemed to come back from sleep and began to look over his tiny house, porch made from different colored wood, flowers growing out of troughs-boxes-pots.

"Yes." He reached slowly and touched the unpainted railing, strong fingers searched along smooth wood. "I built this with Morgan's help. He lives over there." He swung the pop bottle, causing a little foam to run over his hand. The next shack wasn't so nice: broken steps and tin curling up on the roof, no flowers. A ragged Confederate flag hung from a stick at the top of the steps.

"So where's your wife?"

His face went dark again.

"You said she named your dog so I thought maybe she was here too." I switched from stroking Cin to petting Jane, causing her curvy black eyebrows to raise and flatten on each stroke.

When he didn't say anything I said, "I'll bet you don't get bothered here much. Except for trains. Anyway you probably don't get many salesmen banging on your door."

The man laughed, a real laugh this time. He nodded at me and said, "Only the truly desperate. We did have a seed salesman last spring. There are the occasional bible people, publications or join-our-cult. Buck said an encyclopedia representative came by a while back when I was out. You have to respect their dedication."

He seemed all right again now and I wanted to keep him

talking. "Do the railroad people ever come around?"

The man frowned and his jaw started to move back and forth exposing the hollows under his cheekbones and yellow gums, though his face wasn't naturally narrow or long and his teeth were kinda white, and I could tell this wasn't a good subject to bring up.

"Yes," he said finally. "Sometimes." Abruptly he sat forward and looked kind of angry. "They threaten to destroy our homes! Call us *squatters* on their property. But look here," he rose and pointed down over the porch railing. I got up and looked where he was pointing.

"We have sunk piling, you see, into these unstable banks to support our homes. We dug the holes with shovels." His watery eyes started flashing and didn't seem to be directed at the pilings.

"Some of them are quite deep," he continued. "The whole bank is unstable and we have to hold it back from the river. The river wants to take *everything*, you see, and we have held it here, in this place. We have sunk piling. *We* stopped the river from taking the tracks. That would cost the railroad a great deal of money. A great deal."

He was getting kind of weird, spittle in the corners of his mouth, voice higher.

"They know it would cost more if we were not here, yet they persist. They harass. They do not respect what we've done. *We will do our duty if they just leave us alone.*" He waved his hand at the river. "We have held back the force of the water. Buck is an engineer. He has counseled us about sound building principals in unfriendly terrain."

He began moving around the porch as if looking for something. "We know what we're doing here. Anyone with any sense can see it is *us* that has held the destruction back." Waving his arms randomly, root beer spraying out of the bottle. "Not those fools with their maps and stupid calculations! Without us their calculations mean nothing! *Nothing*! It is *we* who face the river. *We* will hold the line! Because of us they . . ." His face suddenly went white. "Because they . . ." The root beer bottle hit the porch.

I half caught him and helped him back down into the chair. He was still trying to wave his arms. "Take it easy," I told him. "Nobody here now. No railroad people around today."

Wouldn't you know with all the commotion his dog started crying again in that high-pitched way and Cindy, poor messed up dog, she tried to get in on helping me get the man calmed down. He didn't fight me off, get actually violent, but the way he thrashed around I had to be careful because I wasn't sure where this was going and figured the situation could change any second, so I had to be ready for whatever might happen.

But then he began to simmer down. He wasn't looking at me, wasn't really looking at anything, hands tense on the chair, mouth pulled down, lots of spit running from his mouth, and a smell from him that wasn't pee or crap or because he hadn't bathed, something more complicated. I didn't know what it was except it *was not* something I wanted to smell. I felt kind of sick then. Time to get out of there. But he'd helped my dog. It was only right for me to stay around until he was straight again, although I wasn't sure what straight for him was. I didn't know anything except he'd helped my dog.

So I used a small towel he had on a line to wipe his mouth, kept him there in the chair, talked to him, listened to him jabber about the river, dogs, Morgan the engineer, the need for warm boots, the outrageous price of groceries, even God. Didn't make much sense, but he sounded sincere. It seemed all to be a mystery to him, like the lack of understanding among railroad people.

But finally the sun was going down and I had to leave.

Every few minutes he'd start shaking, glaring out at the river. I went inside his little house and found a thin blanket. It was neat in there, nothing on the floor, a stove made from a steel barrel with a stack going up through the roof, clothes on hangers or hung on pegs, books on shelves, pictures on the walls. Kind of religious pictures – a couple had horses in them, great snorting horses and men with swords. The pitcher he'd brought out earlier was on the counter next to a glass. I filled the glass.

Though it was still plenty warm I spread the blanket over the man, tried to get him to take some water but he was talking without making sounds and all I did was spill some on his chin. I set the glass within easy reach and spoke to him for a time. Cin licked his hand.

"Anyway," I said rising. "I gotta be going. You just take it easy. Get some sleep if you feel like it. Nobody's going to bother you today." The man looked at me and seemed to understand. He seemed calmer.

"Thank's for helping Cin. I'll stop by in a day or two to see how you're making out."

On the way home I watched my dog, but she was all right, smiling up at me. She was a pretty tough little dog. In our future life I could see us making it as hunters and trappers. Maybe we'd build a little house like the man by the river. Not in this humid mud country of course, up in my home country where the rivers ran clear and the trees were so tall you couldn't see to the top.

I told my mother about Cin falling, mentioned the man and his dog. She pointed her fork and came at me with the usual questions.

"You didn't go with him did you? Go into his house? Accept any food? Drink anything? Look at one of those filthy books?"

"Naw."

It was two days until I got back. I'd been thinking about the whole deal down there and decided to pull my three traps. There was just a rat in one. From up on the bluff I watched the man's house for a time, but he didn't seem to be home so I didn't go down. Anyway, I didn't want to go empty handed.

At the end of the week when I got my paper truck money I bought some things at the grocery store, which I put with some rolls I'd snatched from a restaurant on my boss's paper route. He didn't mind if you took a few things from the early deliveries to restaurants as long as you split with him. They'd leave boxes and bags of sweet rolls and other stuff right at the front door of restaurants before they opened in the very early morning and what I got this time were just French rolls, but their brown crust was delicious after working all night and I could take a bite between slinging papers and wash it down with a Pepsi I'd bought from one of those all night places where you put the coin on the counter and a dead looking person barely picks it up.

Cin and me headed down to the river. But when I approached along the gravelly tracks near the man's house I got a prickly feeling on my neck and stopped. Cin's forehead wrinkled up and her nose twitched. Something wasn't right.

I switched the sack of groceries to my left arm and felt the knife in my back pocket. We proceeded slowly. Torn cardboard and other junk around the steps. Smoke coming out of the stack, though it was hot and too early for supper. From inside somebody started singing a cowboy song.

When we got near the steps a man stepped out on the porch. He waved a quart beer bottle while singing, rocking back and forth. I came a little closer, Cin at my side. He finally saw us and I remembered seeing him from up on the hillside, a scrawny, wild-haired man with a red weasel face.

"What the hell you want, kid!"

"Where's the man who lives here?"

He came to the top of the stairs, his arms bowed out a little, beer bottle swinging. "He don't live here no more. I live here now. That's the way he wanted her, and by God that's the way she is. Now what the *hell* you want?"

"I came to see him. Where is he?"

"*Where?* Hell, kid, Tom's dead! Hamburger! Buzzard food!"

I stared. "Who're you?"

He grinned, showing three teeth. "Morgan Skinner, boy, at your service. Now what you got in the bag there?"

"Where'd he go?"

Morgan's skinny arm and hand made a sweeping jester. "*Where?* Hell, boy, the train. That's what we all choose by and by. Train's always at your doorstep. *Train* always comes. You need only walk a few steps to meet it. And *meet it* Tom did."

He started heavy-footed down the steps, smirking at me, swaying and swinging that beer bottle.

"What about Jane?" I asked, just to say something, hearing Cin's low growl.

"Precious Jane went with him, clutched in his arms. Lovers till the end."

I backed up a step. "Why would he do that? Are you the Morgan from next door?"

"That I am," he said, stepping onto the gravel. "And you must be the kid with the dog he kept yapping about. So what's in the sack?"

"Nothing for you."

"Hey, don't be that way, boy. I was Tom's friend. His best friend."

I backed up another step, Cin backing with me. "So if you were his friend, what was his whole name?"

Morgan held out his arms in a welcoming way, broad grin on his skinny lips. "Why, it was Thomas T. Tomlinson. Came from down the pike a ways at Springfield. Infantry he was, same as me, 'cept I was 99th and Tom was 106th at St. Vith. We had our *taste* of the Ardennes by God. Then on to Paree! Mademoiselles from pillar to post!"

"What's the T stand for?" He was getting pretty close and I had to decide what to do.

"Why, stands for Theron. Thomas Theron Tomlinson. Quite a mouthful, which it would appear is what you have in that sack. Give us a look, boy!"

Morgan came for us, but Cin went for him with a god awful snarl, stopping him long enough for me to get turned and squared into a run. Then I heard her coming behind me, gravel spraying and us running and Morgan running – beer bottle whizzing past my ear and skittering on the gravel and over the bank – but he wasn't going to catch us. He might stay even for a little ways but he couldn't hold our pace for long. We could run fast for as long as we had to, even with a sack of groceries. No wino bastard was going to take anything we had.

Morgan didn't last fifty yards. We ran another hundred, then cut up into the trees and climbed the bluff and worked our way back over the narrow trails we knew so well. Above Mr. Tomlinson's little house we sat looking down at Morgan crashing around like some crazed warrior who'd conquered a castle.

I put my arm around Cin. "He acts like it's his now, but it isn't," I told her. "He's just a crazy wino that'l ruin it. Mr. Tomlinson is gone so it doesn't matter. What happens to it now doesn't matter."

Cin whined, looking down at the little house.

"Don't worry, we'll find another place to hunt. Some place without rats. I don't want you gettin' bit by one."

She gave me the nose to the cheek. Where her nose touched was cool to the warm breeze. I wondered what had happened to Mr. Tomlinson that was so bad it made him stand in front of a train. He was a nice man who was gone and somebody had taken his home and all the things that made it his. Soon it would look like the house next door and all sign of Mr. Tomlinson would be gone forever. It was enough to make you wonder about the advantages of growing up. I thought about some newsreels at the movies: black and bright flashes, a man going by on a stretcher with a cigarette in his mouth. I was too young to go to Korea. People talked about Russia and atomic bombs and at school we practiced ducking under our desks if there was a sudden real bright light. I wondered if I'd end up living in a little shack next to a big brown river.

Me and Cin sat looking at Mr. Tomlinson's house, in shadow now in the dusky afternoon light slanting over the river. It was getting evening muggy and nobody was moving around. It was almost time for working men in sleeveless t-shirts to walk down to the closest tavern with their quart saucepans and get them filled with cold beer to take back and drink on their front steps and talk a little with the others on the steps with their saucepans. These were mostly family men that didn't want to sit in the taverns with single men and crazies and the loud women that were always roaming around. I'd go for a saucepan sometimes for somebody I knew in the neighborhood and never take any money for it because I could see how tired they were. They would have preferred to go themselves. I'd tell the bartender who it was for and they'd just give it to me with a smile, sometimes not even take the forty cents. When I got back I'd usually accept a sip from their pan, maybe two pans, and listen to them talk. The younger ones that hadn't been to a war would talk about the one going on, but the old ones, like Mr. Tomlinson, they never brought it up.

Finally it was time to go.

"Hey, Mom's gonna be impressed when we bring home these groceries. But we won't tell her about Mr. Tomlinson. Anyway, when she sees the groceries she'll think I've gone off the deep end like she always said I would. What do you think?"

Cin gave me that low little woof. She knew her share was in there too.

RHAPSODY

Southern Missouri 1953

Best part of the state, they said. *More huntin' and fishin' in the Ozarks than you've got time for. Just watch out where you're steppin', and watch out double what you say.*

Heading south from St. Louis on the back seat of a Greyhound Bus, Gary Bill talked at length about his Uncle Buck Docker. Gary Bill told me it was OK to call him Doughbelly Docker behind his back, but up front you better call him Good Ol' Uncle Buck, or Stud Buck, or Foxy Buck in reference to his stature in the fox hunting community, which sounded interesting and I inquired about it.

"Fox huntin' is a gentlemen's sport where Uncle Buck lives," Gary Bill said. "It's all different than regular huntin'. Dog breedin' and fox huntin', that's the number one thing down there, and Uncle Buck's a expert."

"How's it so different? Everybody knows they use dogs."

"The methods are all special." Gary Bill ran a hand through reddish hair that crackled in the dry cooled air inside the bus. "And there's secrets involved I can't tell you unless Uncle Buck says so."

"Because you don't know," I accused. "Bet you don't even know what kind of gun they use."

"They don't just use one kind," Gary Bill said in that superior way he liked to slide into. "Each person uses the kind that suits 'em."

"You don't know crap about fox huntin'," I said, expecting this would get a sneer out of Gary Bill and maybe some interesting information.

"Least I been in a circle of men when they was talking about the rhapsody," he said, quiet, like it was a secret.

"Huh?"

Gary Bill relaxed his sneer, leaned back and pretended to look out the window, rotated the toothpick to the other side of his mouth. "It's one of the secrets I can't talk about," he said. "'Specially you being an outsider and not nearly a family member."

"The only reason we're going to Buck Docker's is 'cause they want to get rid of us for the summer," I muttered. "You ain't seen your uncle in years. He probably don't even hunt foxes anymore and don't' want us around either."

The fact of the matter, which Gary Bill was aware of, was that I had an interest in dogs, particularly outdoor type dogs such as those used for fox hunting, having studied their pictures in Outdoor Life and at my great aunt's house, so I was pretty excited about meeting the real thing.

Uncle Buck Docker was not there when we got off the bus. In the small restaurant next to the bus stop Gary Bill looked over the people, shook his head. I batted a fly into the wind made by the big fan in the corner. We lugged our tattered luggage outside to a bench shaded from the June sun.

An occasional car passed by, scowly people in floppy rural hats staring out the window at us. I stared back, switched to a surprised look just to see their noses press the edge of the window before they were gone down the dusty street. Across from us a line of stores looked mostly deserted, except for the steady flow of people going in and out of Brewer's Hardware & Fence Supply. Brewer seemed to be the main merchant in this itty bitty town.

"Prob'ly forgot all about us coming," I offered. Gary Bill didn't respond.

"Big man like that," I continued, "Big Buck Docker. Land owner and fox hunter and all. Breeder of high quality fox hounds. Buck Stud. Stud Buck? Just which end of Buck are we supposed to put Stud on?"

A battered green pickup pulled over, dust swirling in the bed. A thatch of salty-blond hair appeared over the truck's roof, followed by a big, grinning red face with a purple nose any foxhound would have been proud to own. Gary Bill gave a little wave.

"C'mon boys!" Uncle Buck bellowed. "Gary Bill, you have growed like a bean stock. Your momma still that little pretty thing that loves me best?"

Of course I had immediate questions and Uncle Buck seemed pleased to answer. As he drove and talked his belly sort of gripped the lower part of the steering wheel next to where two of his sausage fingers rested.

Uncle Buck said it was a coincidence that I had an interest in foxhounds because he'd already arranged for us to maybe meet some, a kind of treat he referred to it, before he even knew what we might want to do, although he knew boys pretty damn well, having been one, still was in some respects, and he'd bounced Gary Bill on his knee, knew his momma pretty well, knew what she liked, and he damn well knew all about foxhounds even though his personal pack was down to three aging individuals, and he knew the address and nocturnal habits of every fox in the county, just as he damn well knew the worth of every hound in the county, and so on.

But the important part of all his talk was that before we even unpacked we were headed on over to Connelly Little's place to observe state-of-the-art fox hunting hounds during the actual training process, and maybe have a sip a jar. Well, the jar was just for him and Connelly and whatever 'ol boys might be in attendance. Of course I had to ask what was in the jar, not wanting to be cut out of anything important, but all I got was a belly laugh.

Uncle Buck eased the pickup down a gravel drive and we bounced into a yard filled with pens and small shelters with lean dogs tied up around them. As the truck groaned to a stop a couple dogs pointed big eraser noses at the sky and gave out long, mournful howls. I made out four men in wide-brimmed hats and coveralls – two without shirts – a skinny brown and white dog between them, and beyond a squat green and white house.

The men sat on short cottonwood logs in a semicircle around a forlorn young hound with a rope around its neck. This lean dog looked a lot like the pictures I'd seen of foxhounds: random brown splotches and sprinkles over a short white coat, four white feet. But then there was the trembling.

In his left hand Connelly Little had what looked like an old gray sock pulled over a rounded piece of wood. In his right fist he held the hound's ear. He offered the sock to the dog, encouraged him to take it, moving it a little closer. The dog whined and tried to avoid looking at the sock. Connelly persisted, talking to the dog in a gentle way, inching the sock closer. Finally the dog began to ever so slowly open its mouth and reach for the sock. Connelly suddenly twisted the dog's ear, causing it to utter a sharp cry.

"*No,*" Connelly commanded.

I looked at the solemn group of men and realized the procedure would be repeated. The next thing I knew Docker was blocking my view of Connelly and the dog. I guess it was my stricken look.

"It's the best way," Uncle Buck said. "They gotta learn to accept commands from their master. It's for their own good."

I turned away from Connelly Little's training session and walked up to the road.

After a time Docker's pickup came up the drive. I got in without saying anything. Gary Bill and his uncle talked about family matters until we got to his place, which was a little startling at first sight since it looked almost exactly like Connelly Little's place. The green-trimmed white house was more weathered, smaller, on the edge of town instead of outside a ways, and the driveway wasn't sloped so much, but dog houses were there in the front yard. Dogs appeared as we drove down into the yard but they didn't seem very interested in our arrival, all three a little too lean, dusty, dopey, not at all what you'd expect pure foxhounds to be like.

Docker's son, Nathan, was sprawled in a porch chair, looking a lot like the hounds in the yard. We nodded to each other during introductions. I started to extend my hand, but realized it wasn't a situation that called for handshakes. Gary Bill and I sat in the small, cluttered kitchen and ate some hard biscuits and beans Docker offered. A roar out front and I looked through the screen door as Nathan got into a convertible with two other young men. In a low voice I asked Gary Bill directions to the bathroom. His answer was a chuckle. He let me frown at him for a time.

"Two-holer out back," Gary Bill finally said, and right away I wondered if that meant there were two doors to the bathroom. But that isn't what it meant at all. There were spiders and flies in that two-holer, and not much room below the bare wood seats, if you know what I mean.

Later in our small room, where Gary Bill got the skinny bed and I got the skinnier cot, we assessed the situation. Thinking always made Gary Bill's face scrunch up so the freckles across his nose brightened and his greenish eyes hazed over like a traffic light in the fog.

"I think we'll be all right if we just mind our *own* business," Gary Bill said. "There's plenty of stuff to do and a pretty girl lives right across the street. She was watching when we got out of the truck. She probably has a friend'l go for you, if Uncle Docker shears off some a that mane stickin' outta your brush-ape head. Dinky town like this, they'll go for city boys."

"I ain't a city boy."

"You *live* in a city."

"Maybe so, but my *mind* is in the country. And I *have* lived there."

Gary Bill just smiled his sneaky smile.

"What're you up to?" I asked uneasily, suddenly repelled by Gary Bill's worldly ways, wondering if these little town girls were as strange as the men I'd met so far. "We can't mess around like that. You saw how they treat their dogs and they weren't even mad. I don't want to upset any of 'em in that way. We better stick to fishing."

"Oh, we'll do some fishin'," Gary Bill said. "We'll fish and roam and chase foxes all night. They may have sent us down here for penance, but we can turn it into a *real* vacation."

I lay back on the cot and thought about fishing and fox-hounds and what we were into down here next to the Ozarks. I didn't think we were in the real Ozarks because where we were was nearly flat and Ozark country was known to have high hills, although I had noticed some pretty big hills a ways behind Docker's place.

At that time girls were much too complicated. I liked them all right, but they were always cleaned up and pretty and I was like some mountain man after a bad winter. You couldn't blame them for easing back and smiling in a nervous way. But Gary Bill, he even had regular conversations with them, scheming snake that he was. And they flirted with him until he had them eating out of the palm of his hand. That was supposed to be the ultimate deal, to have them eating out of the palm of your hand, like pigeons.

Lying there staring at the mold green paint peeling off the ceiling, I decided to stick with what I knew, which was huntin' and fishin' and most anything outside a town or city. Gary Bill couldn't beat me there. And when it came to dogs it was no contest. Dogs responded to me the way girls went for Gary Bill, no good sneak that he was.

The very next night we went fox hunting. Gary Bill and I had already made a tour of the town, which didn't take long. We found the two-table pool hall and lunch counter, the only ongoing downtown entertainment being offered unless you were to count the pinball machine next to the meat department in the grocery store. There was also the one-eyed man, a veteran of Satan's Saber was how he introduced himself, that came to preach in front of the bank building. But he was heavy into damnation so we didn't hang around long.

That evening after more mushy beans with a small part of a pig in it and some cold cornbread alongside, we headed out across rolling farm country in three old pickups, Docker

following one with rusted-out fenders and a roped-up tailgate. Through moist twilight my eyes followed the tumbled
lines of brushy fence rows between pastures and crop fields,
good places for game to hide. Lots of cover too next to old
split-rail fences and behind broken cars jacked up around
barns. And there seemed to be a lot of those two-holers out
behind clapboard houses.

I had some reservations about the hunt, but decided I
didn't have to agree with all their ways to learn something
about fox hunting. Primed with a couple questions from me,
Docker began jabbering away. The first thing I learned was
there were no firearms involved in southern style fox hunting. It was a gentlemanly sport as it had always been and
still was in England.

"We carry on the old tradition," Uncle Buck said rever-
ently.

I tried to equate the potbellied and one no-belly, sag-ass,
tobacco-chewing men in coveralls bouncing down a rutty
dirt road in beat-up pickups, dogs squabbling and howling
in the back, in relation to the unbelievably dressed horse
riders following a big pack of real spiffy dogs I'd seen in the
picture over my great aunt's fireplace; scrolled into a brass
oval at the bottom were the words, *In Pursuit of the Fox*, and I
used to study that picture for long periods when my mother
took me along for a visit. Now my oldest aunt was not from
around here either, probably didn't even know what *around
here* meant around here, but I just couldn't make these pictures match up, couldn't imagine why these people would
want to identify with the English in their fancy red jackets.
The only red these men wore to the hunt were on the hand-
kerchiefs dangling out the back pockets of their coveralls.
Horses didn't even enter into it. Now the dogs, though, most
of them, they did have similarities, and though they might

not be quite as clean as the English version they were in good voice and ready to go. So there was that. And then there was the fox. We certainly had more foxes than the English. Way more. There were enough red foxes in America to eat all the foxhounds in England, and that's not even counting our silver and cross variations. We had foxes to the point of being a nuisance sometimes, so why didn't they shoot the odd one just so they wouldn't overrun the countryside?

"Happens sometimes with a chicken thief," Uncle Buck said, correcting the steering wheel as the truck bounced and shuddered over more holes and ruts, causing his ruddy jowls to flap like chaps in the wind. "And the dogs will kill one sometimes. It's nature's way. Fox gets old like we all do. Can't run the route no more."

"What's that?" I asked. "Foxes have their own routes?"

"*Well certainly,*" Uncle Buck said, spat a wad out the window, swiped with the back of his hand at the brown streaks running from the sides of his mouth.

"You take 'ol Snake Swimmer. Now there was a good 'ol fox. Chased him for ten year. Had hisself a regular and a special route. Dogs get too close, he'd head for Snake Creek every time." Uncle Buck's deep-set blue eyes twinkled as he forced the tires to straddle a deep groove in the road. The headlights swept over a dead raccoon down in that groove.

"Jump in there below Gar Skinner's dam and swim downstream about a hundred yard," Docker continued. "Sneak out at Grey Rock Point and run right on up that slick rock. Dogs always lost him there. Heck of a smart little runner. Whenever the dogs got to the dam, we'd call 'em in."

"So what happened to that fox?" I asked.

"Got old and slow. Didn't quite make it to Snake Creek one night. Dogs closed and got 'im." Uncle Buck's voice had dropped into sadness.

We stopped on a flat section of dark road. Tailgates were dropped and eager dogs leaped out barking and baying, running around and through the crowd of people. It was a warm night full of crickets, sweet smells and insect flights, and the unseen stirrings in the country at the end of twilight. Murmuring commenced among the men and some kind of consensus was reached. A lanky fellow went across the road, stepped around and through a cattle guard on the fence row and called the dogs with a series of high-pitched clicks. Barking and yipping, the dogs crowded through the narrow fence opening and raced off into the night.

The pack soon found a trail. Intense baying filled the heavy air until you couldn't hear the insects and other night sounds, their voices rolling like giant violins on the muggy air and slicing through swarms of bugs and darting bats.

"That's my Matthew hit scent first," Connelly Little announced.

"Rolle's already in front," said the tall man who had sent the pack off.

"Ol' Sally's steady there in the middle," Docker added. "She's the logical anchor."

"Angling toward Bob's Barn," the fourth man said. "It's that chicken killin' sumbitch Silver Tail again. I hope the dogs get 'im tonight. By God I do."

"Nah," Docker said. "They ain't gonna catch Silver Tail. He'll go through the corral and over a couple haystacks. He'll be a mile down the trail by the time the dogs figure her out."

From the seat of Connelly's pickup a tan gallon crock appeared. The men passed it around, drank by crooking a finger through the neck ring and tipping it over a forearm. Gary Bill and I moved in a little closer and with sly, tobacco-stained grins they offered us a turn.

Being a bold fool I drank first, tipping the jar as the men had done and taking a good mouthful from the crock. As I swallowed there was sudden blindness followed by the realization that my entire mouth and throat were on fire. I was vaguely aware of my eyes trying to burn out of their sockets and men laughing. This was my first taste of white lightning. Everclear. 160-plus proof. Pour it in your gas tank and drive to New York. Pour it down your throat and see Jesus. I handed the crock over and sagged against a fender.

"Maybe I'll pass this round," Gary Bill said.

I sucked it up and swiveled my head to the men gathered around us. "This boy wants to mess with your daughters," I croaked.

"I know your kind," Connelly Little said meanly. "Better drink up, Gary Bill. And if you come round my daughter you'll be hog grub for sure."

Gary Bill drank. His eyes lit up like glow-in-the-dark marbles and he eased over against a tailgate.

The jar went around again as the men talked about the dogs, guessed which way ol' Silver Tail would run next, laced this with gossip about their neighbors. After my second turn with the crock those mournful voices out there in the dark began to blend and separate, surge and almost die out, and I thought I was beginning to understand a little something about fox hunting.

"I think I hear it," I said to Gary Bill.

"Hear what?"

"You know. The music part."

"What damn music?"

"Listen. I hear Sally. And Matthew. He's got the deep voice. And the others. All separate."

Gary Bill stumbled to the side of the road and vomited into the sweet grass growing tall and green in the ditch. His gagging sounds distracted the men from their conversation.

"What's this?" the lanky one said.

"Some people just don't have the stomach for fox huntin'" I offered.

"Well now, that ain't true," Docker protested. "Gary Bill's my own kin. There's fox huntin' in his blood. Gary Bill? What's a matter with you? Was it the beans?"

I have to admit that after another round of jar I wanted to puke too, but I held it in, not about to lose the advantage in this situation to Gary Bill. The gibberish of the men notwithstanding, I could hear the dogs and this was their time, running hell-bent through the dark after a fox that understood too, I sensed that, the fox playing his role, running for his life, a life revered by all these men and dogs for their own private reasons. In England a fox may be the large predator, but not here where they must avoid nearly every other predator. They must be clever and their small, sensitive nose and night eyes must never fail. Losing a pack of hounds in the dark seemed the least of their worries.

Previously I'd seen three foxes in the wild in broad daylight. One dog fox was very close and he paused so we could study each other, as if he was aware I did not have a gun. We were within a hundred yards of the farmhouse and chickens had been killed. He was a beautiful deep red-orange with a bushy white-tipped tail, and he seemed to understand that I posed no danger in that moment. That fox lived a long way from here, but I saw him again that night of my first fox hunt, running confidently before the dogs, knowing exactly where he was going, cutting and dodging through a countryside carved up by humans for their purposes, using it for his purpose. Or maybe *her* purpose? Maybe she had spring kits back in the den, tiny foxes the size of a woman's fist. In that case she would lead the dogs away from the den, just as the male would do, but perhaps her style and route would be different. Would the dogs know this?

"Is this really Silver Tail they're on?" I asked.

"Should be," Docker said. "But he didn't take that turn at Bob's Barn. Into the woods now and headed for Vernon's place. Get's in the corn, the dogs can close."

"Maybe it's Silver Tail's mate," I blurted. The men looked blearily in my direction.

Silence except for baying hounds. I gazed out into the dark and said, "I've seen plenty of foxes in Illinois."

The men started the jar around again. They didn't offer it to me, a minor relief.

"Possible," the man who had sent the hounds out said. "Could be his bitch."

Connelly Little grunted and cut one that momentarily drowned out the hound's voices. "Could be that bitch I invited to the carnival," he said. "Now there was a little bitch could run."

After the husky chuckles quieted Docker said, "Naw, I figure Silver Tail's got too much savvy to let his bitch get in front of a pack a dogs. Just cut hisself a new route. Using that weed patch south a Bob's Barn where the old discus is. Bet he'll try to run the dogs through there. Run 'em into that rusty metal. Sneaky little sumbitch, you can't deny him that."

Mumbles of agreement.

"Old Sally's runnin' second now," Docker said. "Where's that dumbass Matthew now? Makes you wonder if these kids will ever be able to run a whole entire route. By God you can't train the heart in 'em. No offense, Connelly, but it's enough to make you wonder if the breeds deterioratin'."

"I do wonder about that," Connelly Little said. "I'm concerned about it as you are. Most pups I get lately ain't worth the grub we feed them." He stood straight and sighed. "Must a got some bad blood somewhere. Only thing I can figure. Might have to kill the lot and start over before we're through. Sad as it sounds, we could be at the end of a road here."

I tried to just listen to the dogs. There was a change, their voices confused, not moving in any particular direction. "Lost him," one of the men said. "Treed?" another suggested. "Hell no, they're at the creek. He swam fer it. Give 'em the horn, Henry."

The lanky man stepped forward holding a hollowed bull's horn, arms out a little as if to steady himself. With puffed cheeks he blew a long trumpet sound at the sky, then two shorter ones. We waited, looking out at the dark where the night sounds closed in again.

And pretty soon the dogs came running in: Sally, Matthew, Rolle and the rest, six in all, tongues flapping and happy, streaks of sweat on their shoulders and muzzles, mini howls of joy as they ran through the loose cluster of people.

They gathered up Gary Bill where he was sprawled by the ditch and put him in the pickup with me and the dogs. It was a great ride home that night with happy dogs in the back of the pickup, stars and moon blazing down, Gary Bill puking and moaning over the tailgate. Just excited about my first fox hunt with hyper dogs jumping around and licking my numb head.

We didn't get up early.

A strange smell seeped into my nose and under my eyelids, finally caused me to sit up quick. Beyond the worst smell I could imagine for breakfast, and I didn't think it was because I was dizzy. I cracked the door and leaned out.

Docker was in the kitchen with a big galvanized tub on the wood stove, steam curling up, him stirring with a white stick the size of a baseball bat.

I drew back and woke Gary Bill. "Come on!" I urged over his groans, pulling on an arm. "I think your Uncle's cookin' Sally!" He acted like he was in real pain, lazy as usual.

"Sally who? Lemme alone."

"Sally the dog, stupid! This is serious!" I jerked his arm, yanked him right out of bed so he thudded to the floor. He cursed at me, threatened violence, but there was nothing else to do.

Finally I got out of him what was going on, although at first I couldn't believe any part of it. But Gary Bill wasn't fooling. He sat there on the floor and told me his Uncle Buck took in wash. That was his job along with chopping neighbor's stove wood and driving elderly people to the store. He got a small pension for some disability claim that was not enough to survive on, even in a little town like this, and there wasn't any work except at the grain elevator or farm labor which was only available to younger men. So Uncle Buck heated water by the tub-full and washed other people's clothes for a few dollars.

"Nathan gives him five or ten dollars a week," Gary Bill said. "And whenever he threatens to leave Uncle Buck begs him to stay. His wife and daughter left years ago. All he's got is Nathan and fox hunting."

"And the dogs."

Gary Bill shrugged. "I guess they were good dogs once, but they're old now. The only one that can still run with the pack is Sally, and she's about done."

"I need some restaurant coffee," Gary Bill said, pulling himself back up to sit on the bed and resting his head in his hands with his fingers locked in tangled red hair. "Some kinda damn coffee that won't make me feel worse than I already do. You got any money?"

We slipped out and walked the six blocks to the center of town and I bought him a cup of coffee at the pool hall. But then Gary Bill complained the balls banging together was too much to take.

"How come you're so damn spry?" he demanded. "Why should I be the only one to suffer?"

"It's pretty clear why," I said. "You just don't understand fox huntin'."

When we got back I spent some time messing around with those old dogs. They liked the attention but had that scared thing, as if my next move might be something to cause them pain. Finally I convinced them and they were just dogs, you know, full of fun and gentleness with a certain wonder. It got me to thinking how those other dogs were after the hunt.

That same day we found out about Turner's Dam, barely a mile from Docker's place through a nice stand of oak and cottonwood and then a real snaky marshy part with small moccasins everywhere, but we didn't see any big cotton-mouths and no copperheads on the trail. There were lots of baby moccasins you could grab up in your fist and watch them try to bite your hand. Their teeth were too tiny to get the poison in, but the bigger ones, you had to grab them by the tail and snap their necks quick before they could turn and bite. We didn't feel like snapping any necks that day.

A body of water came into view through the willows and abruptly I halted and put an arm up, which Gary Bill ran into before stopping. Two big white crane birds spread their wings and lifted out of shallow water. They angled around to gain altitude, flying together slow-like, and then came right over us. Those birds looked huge, and as they approached I saw the black bands under their wings and recognized what they were.

"We could shoot 'em right out of the air from here," Gary

Bill said. "If we had guns."

"Don't you know what those are?" I said. "They're *whooping cranes*. There was pictures of them in Outdoor Life. See those black bands under their wings? There's only about twenty-five left in the whole world. Man, I didn't know they were so pretty." I gazed up as the great white birds flew over us with wings synced in perfect rhythm. Gary Bill moved past me on the trail, but I kept watching until they were specks in the sky and finally disappeared over a line of trees. It was strange to think I might never see another one of those cranes ever, them being on the verge of extinction. I wondered if they lived around here, or were just passing through. I could imagine people that didn't know what they were taking pot shots at them. And those whoopers flew too slow, a graceful, easy pace to their wings. They didn't have the instinct foxes had. They didn't seem to know they should avoid people even when they were up in the air.

A concrete dam across a little creek formed Turner's Pond, about five acres of lily pads, smart bass and fat bluegills. Below Turner's Pond was another old dam that had broken in the middle and made a series of pools, which we found more productive. We baited up with worms and started catching bluegills the size of a farmer's hand. Sitting on a broken part of the dam, watching my bobber for the next strike, I said, "We should do something for those dogs."

"What dogs?"

I looked over at Gary Bill, half asleep on a chunk of broken concrete, not paying attention. "Your Uncle Buck's dogs. Cooped up like that. They'd like this place."

"They ain't cooped up. They're outside all the time. Fed and housed."

"They're tied up," I said. "Sally's the only one that gets to go hunting."

"That's how things are. Old dogs stay tied up. Young dogs hunt."

I stared at Gary Bill, but he wouldn't take notice.

"Asshole," I said. "You don't understand nothin', you don't see nothin' except girls, and you don't even know you got a bite on your line."

Gary Bill set the hook and his rod bowed. I saw the flashing bluegill down there in the clear water, angling against the pull of line.

"I may not see whatever it is you see," Gary Bill said, grinning, "but I sure would-a seen that big ol' cottonmouth about to swim under my line."

Gary Bill spoke the truth: six feet, triangular head, dark brown back, body big as your wrist and me, being a little off that day, thinking about other matters, raised my wimpy fiberglass pole and slammed down hard across the middle of that big snake, which caused it to rear back and strike at the rod with long, deadly teeth, then at me with pure white mouth full open, just as I pulled my legs out of the way. He tried again and missed and then I was up on the narrow concrete out of the way, scrambling back with Gary Bill laughing and me cursing at that snow-white mouth. We each got a handful of rocks and threw at that snake as he escaped into the jaggy rock bank across the pond.

"Snake huntin' with a fishin' rod," Gary Bill growled. "Only a matter of time till one hits you good and I'll have to watch you croak. One that big hits you, you won't even make it back to Uncle Buck's. Where's all that country instinct gone to?"

I didn't answer, but on the way back I reminded Gary Bill about the dogs. "We have to do something."

"Nothing to do," Gary Bill replied. "Not our dogs. Not our town. Not our business. Best part of our business today is that we'll have fresh fish for supper instead of stale beans. Soon as you clean 'em of course, since I caught the most."

"We got four apiece. And those old dogs still want to hunt."

"You can't start something," Gary Bill warned. "You're crazy as hell and you better not mess with Uncle Buck's dogs. They won't put up with it. This ain't that weird place you come from. These people have their *own* ways."

The very next morning with damp heat already making our armpits sticky and dusty rays angling through the big oak and the sycamore across the street that sheltered a hundred birds, I had Gary Bill out early and we were tearing into the dog's houses when Docker made his appearance.

"What the hell . . ."

"We're just tidying up," I said before Gary Bill could speak. "Just so you won't have to. Cleaning their beds and beating the fleas out. Killin' ticks and maggots so there won't be any disease. I figured you'd appreciate us doing some extra chores around here."

"He took it upon himself," Gary Bill said, arms folded like he wasn't part of it. He hadn't been doing much work anyway.

"Well now . . ." Uncle Buck twisted his big mouth into an upside down horseshoe and opened it into a giant yawn, causing his red face to pouch out at the top as if he had cheekbones as he considered the disarray around his front yard: Gary Bill next to a pile of old bedding, the dogs trying to huddle up, rolling their eyes and shivering, me with a water can in my hand. I smiled into Uncle Buck's frown.

"Well . . ." Uncle Buck nodded slowly, mouth making sounds like a cow chewing. "A little tidyin' ain't such a bad idea. Just don't get too much water on the dogs. They get colds y'know." He turned, looked back, then disappeared into the house.

I turned to Gary Bill who was staring after his uncle. "C'mon," I urged. "Get those dog beds in a pile over by the road so we can burn 'em."

"It's not gonna work out," Gary Bill said, dragging an end of a burlap and straw bed. "They'll turn on us. I'll say it was all your idea. They'll believe me."

Those mangy old beds made a great roaring fire. Fleas flew out like confetti and disappeared by the thousands into the rising smoke and flames. Uncle Buck came charging and woofing out of the house, neighbors were yelling from across the street – scared I guess that sparks would ignite their houses, but it was too late to stop it. All that old burlap and straw and rags and newspapers went up in flames that fried the low leaves of the oak, sent birds flying off, sent those folks scurrying for their hoses and water cans. But by the time they got squared away the fire was coming down.

The dogs were bug-eyed with all the yelling and fire and I crouched down and hugged Ned, the oldest dog, felt him trembling as we watched his bed and the others burn into wispy ashes.

Sure there was some confusion and anger, but I mostly convinced the neighbors that me and Gary Bill, Buck Docker's own nephew, were just trying to clean things up a little and get rid of any potential disease that might be ready to hatch.

"Wasn't my idea at all," Gary Bill cut in, and I gave him a look – which worked that time – and we set about completing the task. We washed the doghouses inside and out with Docker's strong detergent. Then we washed the dogs. Docker was into his jar by then so we got those dogs all clean and prancing around before he even noticed. Daisy and Sally became fine with these new events, but Ned, he couldn't get into it. His hound's forehead was all wrinkles and his mouth clucked like he had loose dentures and his eyes couldn't stop weeping. But at the same time he seemed to be enjoying the attention. There was just too much activity reflected in his old eyes. I sat down with him and listened to his low whine, continuous, like a telephone with nobody there, stroked his skinny-shivery back and scruffy fur, resented his trembling, resented the cause of it.

The next day I got Nathan to bring fresh burlap bags from the elevator. That same afternoon, down the street, I met a big blinky-eyed lady who said she'd give us some straw she'd bought for her sheep if I would shoot two blue jays that had killed a cardinal right in her yard and taken over the bird pond. I told her I'd do it if I had my rifle. She went into a closet and came out with a single shot .22 and five cartridges. It was a Remington like mine, except older.

I missed with the first round, the rifle shot low and a little left. The next one hit the mark. That jay fell straight without a flutter and the mate flew off. I fired a round into the tree, then went in the house and told the lady I'd shot both those jays. She gave me the straw. Gary Bill and I made the new beds and cleaned up the yard a little. The dogs looked better, but it didn't seem enough.

"You've reached the end of your rope," Gary Bill said. "I'm not going to join you on the end of it. I've got a date with Linda, that blond across the street. Her friend Betty might have went with you, but you didn't hang around. Me and Linda are going down to shoot some pool."

"Betty already said she wanted to go with me. I told her we'd whip you and Linda's butt."

Gary Bill looked startled, then his eyes narrowed down to greenish slits.

"The thing about fox hunting," I said, wanting to extend

any momentary advantage over Gary Bill, "is that when you take away the ol' boy crap it's about the dogs. And the fox. And the country. It isn't really about the people."

"That's stupid!" Gary Bill shot back. "Without the people there wouldn't be any fox huntin'."

"Yeah. I've been thinking about that. What it's about. You know in brush a fox is quicker."

"Maybe, but not in the open."

"Yeah," I countered, "even in the open for a short ways. A fox can turn into a streak. He may be little, but he's wild. That's his edge. He makes his living out there for his family and himself. In the open he can outrun anything for a short ways because he has to."

"So what if he can? So what if he can run up a tree or slick rock, or run a creek until he jumps ten feet up a bank to lose the dogs? So what if he can swim underwater to catch a duck? He's a fox doing fox things. The people and dogs are doing their own things. Now you come along and want to disrupt what's been worked out over generations of fox huntin'."

I enjoyed Gary Bill's frown for a while, sensing it was one of those times when I might get him to do something he would never consider doing himself.

"Got nothing against fox huntin'," I said. "Just don't like the entire part the dogs play in it. Buncha ol' doughbelly Bucks beatin' on dogs to make em' chase a fox through night woods and spend the rest of the time tied up or in a cage. How good at running would a fox be if he was tied up for ninety percent of his life?"

Gary Bill straightened into a glare. "He'd prob'ly be no good as a sporting animal, which could be the point your missing. The fox has to be wild and the dogs have to be owned and trained by people or the sport don't make no sense. Foxhounds don't chase poodles or polecats. It's a specialized thing. Goes back even before America. Hell, it started in England."

"Yeah. Fifty dogs jumping over those little stone walls they have over there and all those guys in red jackets riding beautiful horses. It always struck me as a fun-dumb thing to do."

"So?" Gary Bill said impatiently. "What's your problem?"

"I just can't help wondering," I said. "You suppose old Ned's ever seen Turner's Pond?"

"If Uncle Buck wanted Ned to see Turner's Pond," Gary Bill said evenly, "then he's seen it."

"Maybe," I said, in a way I hoped would be irritating. I guess I was irritated too. All this fox hunting business caused me to keep seeing that red fox in the last state I'd lived in, so close I saw the breeze tickling the black hairs on his ear tufts, looking at me straight as an animal can look for a lot longer than he had to and I forgot about my rifle.

We did all go to the pool hall, Gary Bill, Linda, Betty and me. About a game and a fraction into the contest I asked Betty if she'd ever been fox hunting. "Of course not," she said, pulling down tight dungaree shorts over tan legs, "it's what men do."

"What about dogs?" I asked hopefully.

"What about them?"

"Do you like 'em?"

Betty brushed a wave of chestnut hair away from her eye and for the first time, it seemed to me, gave me a direct look. She did have a sweet round cute face. "I have a beagle pup named Lady," she said.

"Oh, a beagle." I nodded, smiled. "They're nice little dogs."

"Yes. Lady is very nice. She's just four months but she already has perfect markings."

"You gonna teach her to hunt rabbits?"

Betty frowned at me. "That's what everyone asks. But I don't think so. Lady is special."

"Oh, so you want to make her a specialty tracker. Opossums and coons?"

"No," Betty said, pretty firmly in her soft voice, "I want to show her."

"Show her what?"

It was before we lost that second game of eight ball to Linda and Gary Bill that I realized I wasn't doing very well. Betty was a really cute girl and she had those bubbly lips they call kissable, and surely they were, but I wasn't confident of my technique in that area and feared embarrassment. She was also a lousy pool shooter.

On the way back, the four of us walking two by two, Betty offered that the carnival was coming in less than three weeks and me, being a fool, I asked if she usually went with her family. Though you could say I didn't get the drift, Gary Bill became the bigger fool by inviting Linda right then, said he'd take her up on the Devil's Whip, which was a ride at a St. Louis amusement park and had nothing to do with this small town carnival. Besides, I didn't have but eighty-four cents to my name and Gary Bill had eighty-four cents less than I did. About then Linda turned to us and said we should all go together, it would be fun, to which Betty said, "Sure."

Later, stretched on our skimpy bunks, we hashed it back and forth and decided the only option open for meeting our social obligations was to pick blackberries and sell them. There were acres of wild blackberries all over the place just coming ripe, but anybody with the money would rather pay somebody else to pick them. At that time the grocery store in town was selling blackberries for fifty cents a quart, a depressed price beyond our control. We figured we could stand outside the store and peddle our blackberries for forty cents a quart. We were strangers in town selling unwashed fruit and had to offer some incentive over store prices, even though ours might be fresher. We calculated that selling twenty-eight quarts would put us in a reasonable position to entertain the girls, and who knew where that might lead?

The next morning came real early. We left Docker's place with just the top branches of the old oak in the front yard catching the first rays. We had pancake sandwiches to sustain us and a half-gallon of well water, and we hit that blackberry patch with a plan and determination.

We went high for the biggest, juiciest berries, low for the droopys other pickers wouldn't bend for. By midday you could play tick-tack-toe on our arms. Our faces looked like we'd been whipped with barbed wire. Bees attacked us for muscling in on their territory, or maybe they just wanted the scabby blood. We fought them off and kept picking. A copperhead came up out of dark cover and took a swipe at Gary Bill. He lost half a quart of berries during evasive moves. The snake slithered off and we picked up the berries. In the heat of the afternoon we no longer spoke to each other, just cursed blackberries. That night we ate Uncle Buck's gruel and fell into bed.

"We didn't make it even halfway today," Gary Bill muttered. "I got about six quarts and you three."

"I picked better'n seven and you know it slacker ass."

"Those damn blackberries are under-priced," Gary Bill declared. "Should bring three-four dollars a quart. You can't pick 'em for the going rate. It's slavery, man! Linda ain't *all* that great, ya know?"

"Shutup," I said, too tired to even sound mad. "We shoulda stuck to fishin' and dogs."

"Dogs have nothing to do with this deal – what the hell you bringin' dogs in now for? We're dealing with women here. Just pick your share, 'stead a daydreaming into slow motion."

"Hardest *you* ever worked," I shot back. "Just in the hopes of a feel. All you're likely to get at best and prob'ly not that. Linda doesn't have much in the tit department anyway. One a them slow developers. Stuck up little no-tit-small-town-flower. You talk a lot of crap, Gary Bill, but I doubt you ever did half the things with girls you say you did. Struttin' around like some Uncle Buck doughbelly-stud-cowboy relation that won't even get the time of day when the money runs out."

Gary Bill didn't answer. He was asleep.

Something happened that night. It may have been the ripped flesh, the after hours of feeling those thorns. Could have had something to do with the June heat or Docker's afternoon ravings about fox hunting and great hounds of the past and what a helluva stud he'd continually been until nearly the present, still could be given the right situation, though it was unlikely in these times of low appreciation and under-performing dogs and the wailing of two and four-legged bitches. All the real men and great dogs were dissolving into the swamp muck they'd sprung from, not a hairy ball in the lot, but by God he'd not slide down that path, not Big Ol' Buck Docker, no sir, Buck Docker still had some virgins to fry, hounds to learn the tradition, and so on.

Or it may have been that I was just pissed off about the dogs. Ten feet of rope and a crappy house. Summer heat, winter wet, junk food and a few burnt-up beans a day. I just didn't like it. So the next morning, over Gary Bills protests, I untied Ned's rope from his house and we took him along to the blackberry patch.

Old Ned was all splotchy folds and wrinkles around his

sad brown eyes. He knew he shouldn't be going with me that morning and kept surveying the ground ahead for his usual diversion of insects, ants being the most common although any crawly thing would do. Once it was fox scent – now insects on the ground. He'd let them crawl over his legs and paws with his nose only an inch away. Down between his eyes, over his muzzle to his big corrugated nose, then he'd sneeze them into flight patterns around the yard. He never crushed them or ate them the way some dogs do. Watching him those evenings in Docker's front yard I came to see the insects as Ned's company, any company besides the other two dogs who were in the same situation he was in. Sally, his daughter, still went hunting, which meant he could barely look at her. Daisy hunted sometimes, but she was goofy without cause, like her best sense had been taken away long ago. Most evenings I'd go out and sit next to Ned, stroke his bony head and back until he leaned against my leg. And he would fall into fitful sleep.

So now on the way to the blackberry patch Ned kept up the whine, rolling those old hound's eyes and shivering like a cold wind was hitting his skinny butt.

"Don't worry about it," I told him. "Nothing to do but walk around a little, see what you can see. We'll just be picking berries."

That whole day of hard picking I'd look up once in a while to check on Ned. He never ranged beyond forty yards. Sometimes I saw his whippy tail do the scent quiver above the grass. "Get 'em," I'd yell, and his head would jerk up. He'd make a cartoon smile and his head would go down again and I'd hear snuffling noises.

Gary Bill was so mad about me bringing Ned he wouldn't talk or look at me, but I didn't mind. There were lots of big, ripe berries and we got some work done. About midday we

ate beans and fatback we'd scrounged from Docker's kitch-
en, blackberries from our buckets, washed everything down
with well water. Birds fluttered and chirped all around us,
bugs buzzed and whished past our heads.

The peaceful sounds allowed me to do some thinking,
and I came to a conclusion about the girls I figured would be
unpopular with Gary Bill, so I decided to save it for a better
time. The sun was behind the trees when we headed back to
Docker's, but we had our berries, close enough to twenty-
eight quarts total. We were too tired to care. So was the dog,
trailing along behind with flappy lips practically dragging
the ground.

Gary Bill muttered something about Ned, expecting the
worst, but it was a strange turn of events we walked into:

Fighting in the front yard, people hopping around cursing,
dogs slamming against ropes, shouts from across the street,
Docker bellowing as he lurched down the porch steps. My
first take on the situation was just a regular drunken brawl,
nothing to get too concerned about. But Nathan and some
guy were going at it pretty hard while another young man
and girl watched, these spectators pressed in with encour-
aging words, but it wasn't clear who they were pulling for.
Arms and legs flew and pumped. The fight careened over
Sally's doghouse and into a cloud of dust on the other side.
Nathan took a good punch to the head, rocking him back.
About then Docker came rushing with a pail of water he
threw on the two boys, abruptly stopping the punching.

"Now what the hell's this all about!" Docker demanded.

"'Bout bein' pissed at that sumbitch!" Nathan yelled, spitting water and blood. "Took my *last* beer today and told my
woman *he'd* take her to the carnival."

Docker's eyes became puffy slits. "That true, Leonard?"

The man wiped a torn sleeve across his mouth, muttered,

"He didn't take her out but once."

"But Nathan took her first? Showed her a good time?" Docker glared at the spectating man and woman. "What the hell's your interest in this, Eton?"

"Uh . . ." Eton began.

"Me and Eton and Leonard just come by to see Nathan," the girl blurted. She was thin and stringy-haired with a red halter-top tied off around her neck. Eton nodded.

"Me'n Eton thought we'd stay for the fight," she added.

Docker's gaze moved back to Leonard. "There's a question been put to you, boy."

"Well . . . Nathan only took her over to Springerville for a hot rod party."

"You damn well know what this ads up to, Leonard," Docker said. "Nathon didn't wine and dine this woman so's you could come in and reap the rewards. Matter of fact, it's beginning to sound like that Trudy Sass bitch." Leonard's head and Nathan's both dropped as if they suddenly saw something important on the ground.

Docker shook his head. "Sure it was, sure as hell, you dumbass boys." He turned to Nathan. "I told you to leave that no-account tribe alone. That's a *diseased* family. Old man Sass crazy with the fever."

"I got rights too!" Leonard blurted. "I'll take my women where I find 'em!"

Docker stepped forward and slapped Leonard across the mouth, knocking him to the ground.

But quick as a weasel Leonard grabbed a piece of stove wood the dogs had chewed and came up fast and hit Docker on the side of the head with a solid thonk. Docker crashed down like a broke-leg horse, dust puffing up.

Nathan was on Leonard, ripping the wood out of his fist and pounding him with it, the skinny girl screeching, dogs howling and trying to get out of the way, Eton and the girl jumping into the middle of it all and everybody rolling around in the twilight yard so you didn't know who was on what side.

Big Jim came running and cursing from across the street and Gary Bill cowered back, Big Jim being Linda's daddy, but Big Jim's only intent was to stop the commotion. He kicked some butts and sent them all scurrying off into the muggy evening, Nathan too. Engines cranked up and tires spun gravel.

We then gathered to stare down at Buck Docker lying there in the middle of the yard, wheezing spit from his mouth and nose. Big Jim turned his owly eyes toward Gary Bill and me and we sort of came to attention.

"Better get him inside," Big Jim told us, his heavy brow furrowed and jaw askew. "Get some cool towels on his forehead. If he's alive in the morning, he'll prob'ly live."

"*Yessir,*" Gary Bill said. We watched Big Jim walk back across the street and slam the front door of his house.

Gary Bill turned to me. "How we gonna get him inside?"

I shook my head at the giant mound of Buck Docker, turned toward the moan of dogs behind me. Ned lay in his usual spot next to his house, though I hadn't hooked him to the rope, head on paws, trying to be disassociated from all this craziness. I felt the same way, but here we were.

"Guess we could get some of those smooth boards from the backyard," I said. "See if we can slide him on up the steps."

We soaped those boards with Docker's brown smelly bars. Used more boards as levers. Strained with all we had to move him up. About halfway Docker slid off the boards and lay sprawled on the worn steps. The yellow porch light on the sheen over his face and bare gut hanging to one side made him look dead already. I sat down, ready to give it up, but Gary Bill pleaded, "He's my uncle, man!"

Yeah, shit. So where the hell's Nathan?

Somehow we did it, sweat pouring off us, pulling, straining, rolling, dragging that buck mountain of Buck Docker in the house and onto blankets spread in the middle of his little living room with wet towels on his head. They were customer's towels, but we didn't care. Docker's heaving mass in the house on his own damn blankets. Towels cold and wet on his head. Let God take it from here.

During the early morning we took turns changing cool towels on Docker's head and throat. About nine a.m. a customer came for their wash.

"Got a fever," Gary Bill told the woman. "Took a bad hit last night. Come back tomorrow."

"*Fever*!" the woman squealed. "Buck's got the fever!" She turned and clomped off the porch. "My linens diseased! *Diseased!*" She wailed all the way to her old station wagon.

"Uncle Buck may lose a customer or two over this," Gary Bill said.

"Right now he don't care," I said. "He just keeps jabberin' wantin' his momma to come home and tell him where all the wild pussies went. Did your uncle used to keep wild cats?"

Gary Bill just looked at me.

Nathan shuffled in about the middle of the day, but there was no talking to him. He disappeared into his room.

Docker woke up in the regular sense that afternoon. He demanded food and water. Then some jar, which we respectably refused him. Then he wanted an accounting of events. He didn't seem to care much for how the real story was going so I added a few details out of my imagination, just for his peace of mind. My version didn't set too well with Gary Bill, but he kept his mouth shut. We got his uncle all fed and relaxed and satisfied with the way things were going. He'd been injured saving his son, and he should recuperate before tackling his daily chores.

This appeared like it might be the opportunity I'd been watching for. My personal plan was simple enough, and was geared to family relationships as they'd been explained to me by a person I'd met, a poor but seemingly wise fellow I'd encountered one day while fishing, about being born into debt and playing the lines you were dealt as best you could. There were short and long lines. Saturday night was a short line. The house or farm was a long line. I figured Buck Docker and me could play the kind of short line a non-family person could qualify for. Gary Bill didn't care about lines one way or another and I just told him he'd make out if he played along without helping too much.

The next morning I got up real early and lit a fire in the stove. I started the coffee in one corner and put the wash-tub over the main cast iron lids, filled the tub from the hose that ran from the cold water tap, which was the only tap. This was the same procedure we used for our twice a week baths. That coffee pot looked tiny next to the galvanized tub. A little smoke puffed around the edges of the top plates and the fire inside huffed and grew fast, heating all that cast iron.

I heard Nathan get up.

"Coffee done?" he asked, a rumpled voice and shape in the other room. I shook my head and he went out. His old Ford rumbled and gears ground.

The coffee finally perked. I poured some in one of the heavy mugs that hung under the cupboard, got down a few burning swallows while sizing up the big white sacks full of wash lined up by the back door. Then I started in with a load of stained, wrinkled sheets, forking them into the warm tub water with one of the bleached sycamore sticks the way I'd seen Docker do it. I shaved off some brown soap into the tub. Then I started stirring those sheets around in the steaming water. The strong soap smell rose and got stuck in the sweat on my forehead. It wasn't the worst job I'd ever had. Hot is all, not very interesting. It got less interesting as the morning wore on.

Eventually Gary Bill slouched out to the kitchen, looked over the situation, poured himself some coffee.

"S'pose," he said. "You think this is funny?"

I shook my head. "Not very funny."

"You just take it upon yourself to move in on a man this way? Take over? And you not even kin. Men have been shot for less."

"Go wake up," I told Gary Bill. "What I said still goes. Just do your little part."

"Don't even know what my part is." Gary Bill leaned closer. "You understand we got berries to sell? Women to take somewhere? A payoff for the suffering."

I waved him off. "We'll sell the berries, but I ain't spending all my money on Betty at the carnival. They'll just take our money and dump us for local boys. Even if your charms work with Linda you'll have her daddy to answer to, and he's big as Buck Docker and no doubt meaner. You do what you want, but I'm not spending my few dollars in twenty minutes and go the rest of the summer broke."

"Is this the lousy scheme I'm supposed to like?" Gary Bill demanded.

"Has almost nothing to do with the overall scheme. I'm just being cheap so's I can buy you a cup of restaurant coffee after Linda takes all your money."

"I'll *get* my money's worth," Gary Bill said, and took his coffee out to the front porch. He was mad right then, but I figured he'd come around. Gary Bill was not a morning person. All you could do in the morning was plant a seed and let him chew on it until noon.

Docker's wheezing got louder, then faint cries for help. I took a cup of coffee into his bedroom. He was trying to side-saddle out of bed, big knot above his left ear, one fat knee a-quiver as his foot tested the floor.

"Take it easy," I said, pressing the mug into his hands.

"There's things must get done!" Docker's watery blue eyes staring like he wasn't sure who I was, mouth pulled back like someone expecting to get hit.

I coaxed him back up on the bed while keeping the coffee cup upright. "Your neighbors are concerned about you. They say you should recuperate."

"Neighbors?" Docker's gaze wandered uncertainly around the room. "My neighbors hate me," he said, as if to himself. "Except Florence. But she don't care much one way or 'nother since she went over the edge and started eatin' starlings." His attention settled back on me. "There's chores need to be done," he said. "If I don't do my work I'll lose the house and land and everything."

Docker's scared eyes dropped to his unsteady grip on the coffee mug. I can't say I liked Buck Docker much, but in that moment I felt a certain sympathy for his situation and also was pretty sure my scheme would be all right. In the end I figured no one would mind or get hurt over it.

"Don't worry about the wash," I said. "I'm covering for you there. It'll get done. The dogs have been fed and watered. Everything's taken care of."

"What about Nathan? Is he eating here?"

"He's all right. Just this morning he asked about you. I said you were getting better and he seemed happy about that. He went off to work as usual."

Docker's jowls tensed. "He didn't shoot Leonard, did he? For what he done?"

"Naw. He said Leonard was sorry. Didn't mean to hit you so hard. Said the beer took his head."

"Well." The bed creaked as Docker settled down on stained pillows. "Things are not as bad as I imagined. Things are humming along, thanks to you and Gary Bill. My prayers have been answered. I'm Lutheran you know. Did you know I was Lutheran?"

"No I didn't."

"Are you shaving in the soap after the water's good and hot?"

"Yes I am."

"And stirring? You have to stir the whole time."

I nodded.

"But you're not stirring now and I can smell the wash."

"Then it will get extra damn stir time to make up for the lack," I said. "Look, I'll take care of the chores and I won't take any money. But you have to agree to something."

"What's this? What the hell do you *want?*"

"A fox hunt."

Docker snorted. "I already took you on a fox hunt. That ain't no big deal."

"I want to have a say in the next fox hunt. I want some things my way."

"*What?* You think you know somethin' about fox huntin'? Want to dictate the way things should be! Who the hell you think–"

"You want me to do the wash or not?"

One of Docker's bushy gray-blond brows cocked up and the other eye narrowed. I waited until he looked like he was about to say something, then I talked first. As I told him what I wanted he began to calm down. Finally I asked if he'd like some more coffee. He looked down at the mug, then up at me. I reached over and he gave me the mug.

I finished that load of wash and got everything hung up on the lines crisscrossing between posts in the backyard.

Gary Bill was anxious to go then, so we rinsed out the empty quart milk bottles we'd swiped in the neighborhood to go with the ones we found around Docker's place and started pouring in our berries. We washed a few berries to top off the containers with so they'd all look clean and shiny. Then we headed for town with our merchandise in Docker's rusty old tippy wheelbarrow.

It wasn't so easy to unload those berries, even at our cut-rate price. The people coming and going from that grocery store – women mostly – all seemed excessively suspicious. They could see our raked arms sticking out of our t-shirts and the scabs on our faces and necks. I don't know what they thought we could be up to except selling berries. We'd sold about half our stock when the store owner came rushing out and started yelling at us, calling us scabs, but I don't think he meant the ones on our bodies.

We moved our operation a block down the street to Brewer's Hardware and Supply. Brewer's clientele were mainly men and less suspicious. It was nearly noon and they were hungry. We sold the rest of our berries in no time.

"Let's get a soda and shoot some pool," Gary Bill said.

"I sure could use a soda," I said. "But then I got to get back to the wash."

Gary Bill shook his head, pushed red strands away from sleepy eyes. "You're too weird, man. Think I'll see if I can get some hick in a game of eight ball."

I did the wash on that wood stove. After every third load I dipped the water out in a bucket and poured it down the drain that just emptied into a gravel ditch alongside the property. Started over then with the hose from the faucet. I swept dust over cracked, black-spotted linoleum and out the back door. I brought Docker food and coffee and at first even a bedpan, but I caught onto that pretty fast, told him exercise was good for what ailed him and he'd have to make it to the outhouse on his own. We compromised, his big arm a wet log around my shoulders, grunting-wheezing-shuffling his way out the back door and teetering down the worn steps to the dirt path that led to the two-holer.

It was getting pretty full, so one day I had to carry the container of lye out and pour so much in each hole, according to Docker's instructions. The flies moved back and so did I from the fumes and stink of it all. The lye hissed and ate what was down there, made the top part disappear somehow, made the mass lower so you didn't have to look first before you sat down. I don't know how long this system had been going on, didn't ask.

Late afternoons and after supper were my times.

I'd take the dogs out to a field about a stone's throw behind Docker's place. Gary Bill didn't share my interest in the dogs so it would just be me and whatever dog I'd take along. I only took one at a time and always started with Ned. The others were younger; dogs notice those things. Ned was hesitant at first, just like when we'd gone berry picking, but each time we went to the field there was less hesitation. There were rabbits and mice in the field, sometimes bobwhite quail along the far edge; you'd hear their whistle even if you didn't flush any. But I didn't encourage Ned or the other dogs to go after any animals or birds available there. Until the day I found tracks in a soft sandy spot in the bottom of the little ditch that ran along next to a fence row. I studied the lay and where the tracks were headed, imagined this field at night, looked over behind Linda's folk's place where their chicken house was, and not far along the neighbor's chicken and duck house. It seemed like the best approach. This fox made his living along the fringe of where the people were, picking up scraps and the occasional easy kill.

"Come on over here," I told Ned.

That dog stuck his nose down and snuffled around in those fox tracks until his raggy ears drew swirls in the sand all around them. Then his muzzle pointed straight up at the sky and gave as nice a scent howl as you can imagine. And again, *a-woo-oo, WOO-oo, a-WOOO-oo.* The others heard Ned and joined in from their tethered places in Docker's yard. So I went back and got them too and had all three dogs in the field without ropes around their necks, running free. They wanted to go after that fox and I got a little scared there, trying to bring them under control. I had to yell at Sally to bring her back, which scared Daisy, old Daisy cowering down at my feet in that way I hated. And then Ned sat back and gave us a howl that stopped everything. He was just howling for joy and he kept telling them until they were howling too.

I got them to shush finally. After getting them tied up, I slipped inside quiet like and got a fire going in the stove, started cutting potatoes for supper.

"What the hell's going on?" Docker yelled as I mixed bacon chunks in with the potatoes.

"Nothin'." I poured the whole mess into the frying pan on the stove and started stirring.

"I heard dogs talkin' scent," Docker called from his room.

"There's a chicken killin' fox been cuttin' over in back of your place," I said, pouring in a little bacon grease, stirring. "He must be around this evening. You want a little more jar before supper?"

"Oh, I don't know. How long you think it'll be?"

"Plenty of time." I started cutting an onion to put in with the potatoes and bacon.

"Well. I guess. A little more wouldn't hurt. You get the wash out today?"

"All done," I said. "Collected from Misses Bietch."

"That's nice. Bietch the bitch. You put it up in the jar?"

"Yes I did."

"Gary Bill out there helpin'?"

"He's around."

"You're good boys," Docker said sleepily. "I wish Nathan would take an interest in things the way you boys do."

There was no end to the baskets and bags of wash stacking up on the back porch, just like there seemed to be no end to Docker's recuperative process. That brown soap was making me sick to the point I could hardly eat at mealtime. I just smelled and tasted soap in everything. The one time I saw Betty during that time, over at Linda's, she just turned up her nose and moved a little further away. Women came to Docker's back door and collected the clean wash, patted my cheek, gave me two or three dollars, which I put in the green fruit jar in the cupboard. It seemed business was increasing. On the fifth day I told Docker it was over, he was well enough to resume his duties.

"But the women like you," he said. "How 'bout if I give you forty-cents a tub full?"

I shook my head. "One more. I'll do it one more day. But then we're going huntin' the way we agreed on. If you can't go we'll miss you and talk about you all the way home, how much we missed you not being there."

Docker smiled. "A husky, enterprising lad like you could make some good money to take home to the city. Get you in shape for football. You play football?"

It was a last ditch effort. I just shook my head.

Docker got me to do the wash two more days. Then the night came. We headed out a dirt road past those small farms. Ahead in the first truck was the man that blew the steer horn, Henry Yeager and his oldest hound, Colt. Henry's dog sat right up front in the middle of the seat this night, ears flapping in the breeze from the open windows of the pickup. In our truck were the three of us in front and the hounds in back: Ned, Daisy and Sally. Ned was standing up with his toenails scouring the top of the cab, testing all the rich scents rushing at him.

"Don't expect this to be anything like a regular fox hunt," Docker said. "These old dogs can't run a whole route. 'Cept Sally, but she'll stay with Ned."

"That's all right," I said.

"We'll take 'em over back a Chad Meyer's place. That's Jump Off Jack's territory. Might not even be around now, though I doubt any hound ever caught that ol' boy. Mighta died a plain old age. He'd be over ten now. Killed more'n his share of ducks in his time, that's for sure. Had a hankerin' for big, white tame ducks. Might have been the oil in the meat. It's good for the kits, you know."

I watched Dockers big face jiggling in the lights from the dash, Gary Bill between us looking bored. "Why'd they call him Jump Off Jack?" I asked.

Docker chuckled, spit a wad out the window. "Had to do with his tree climbin' ability. Not just the climbin' but the use of the skill. See, there was this old lightning-split oak by Mossy Creek, at the edge of Meyer's place. And Jack, when there was hounds runnin' him, that little fox would climb up in that tree and scoot across a limb that went over the creek. He'd go right to the end of that limb and jump off clear the other side of the creek and the poor dogs, they'd think he was up in that tree. Drove the dogs crazy for years. Us too, till we finally went over there one night. Jack'd killed a prize duck Meyer's daughter was raising for the 4H, and Meyer, he was determined to kill that fox, promised his daughter, so we followed the dogs with shotguns. That's when we figured out what ol' Jack was doin'."

The truck hit a big hole in the road, raising us off the seat. I looked through the back window to see if the dogs were all right, but mostly I saw Ned's belly. He was still standing up, gripping the top of the cab, toenails raking back and forth and nose into that rich air spilling over the cab.

"So what happened?" I asked.

"Nothin'," Docker said. "Jack was gone. Sittin' out there somewhere laughin' at us. Meyer swore he'd git the little sumbitch, but he never did."

"Did Ned ever run Jump Off Jack?" I asked.

Docker didn't answer right away. Finally I looked over. I thought he might be smiling.

"When we first started with Jack," Docker said. "It was Ned led the pack."

The truck ahead stopped and Henry Yeager got out. In the headlights we watched him open a gate. He got back in and we followed his truck into the pasture and stopped. Eyes glowed at the edge of the lights and cattle wheezed and grunted. The still night air was heavy with the nursery smell of cattle, rank overtures of nearby pigs, oil from the trucks, grass and blooms. June bugs whizzed past like baseballs, fireflies blinked little beacons in the dark beyond the cast of a kerosene lantern that silhouetted a corncob pipe, a dog's perked ear, fence row bramble with bright stars above.

I imagined the fox out there, saw Jack's old nose twitching, reading, calculating the challenge behind all this silly commotion. How good were these dogs? Need he go now or wait a bit to lead them on a trail of no harm? Could this be the night a hound smart enough and fast enough would catch him? Leap upon him with flashing teeth after miles of diversionary tactics?

"Take 'em out, Henry," Docker said.

Henry stepped to the edge of the light and blew a mournful wail out of that horn and those old dogs were climbing all over each other to be gone. Docker chuckled. "Don't have to use the horn for these old rascals," he said. "But they miss it. Gives 'em a git-up charge."

We waited. The jar appeared in the familiar crock, went around. I refused my turn and walked out to the edge of the uneven light cast by the lantern. Gary Bill tipped the jar and made faces, getting Docker and Yeager chuckling.

"Hard to believe he's your kin," Yeager said.

"Ain't it the truth," Docker agreed. "It's that city life. Concrete and cobblestone drains the life out of a man. Have a little more, Gary Bill, you'll get the hang of it."

More chuckles.

The first scent call came. And it was Ned like I hoped it would be, that old deep bass, like dragging a railroad spike around inside a metal drum. He got a good song started before the younger females overwhelmed him with hot scent howls that lit up the night. And they were off.

"Ned hit first," I said.

"I know it," Docker said in a low voice, causing me to look back at him. "You been messin' with that dog," he said. "You got him primed for this."

"He wanted to go."

The dogs were in full voice and I knew them, except for Yeager's hound, Colt, but he was the fourth voice, running third. Sally out front, Ned, Yeager's hound, Daisy bringing up the rear. Docker appeared next to me. We squinted out at the night.

Suddenly those hound's voices gained intensity, a new frenzy in there.

"Jumped him near the creek, up there by Scooter's Pipe." Docker let out a wheezy breath. "It's a damned hot trail now."

In the corner of my eye I could see Docker was concerned about something.

"Want me to try the horn?" Yeager said.

Docker was quiet. Then he said, "No. Wouldn't hear it anyways. They're too close to him."

We listened to the dog's clamoring cries and desperate howls. They were moving away.

"You think it might be Jump Of Jack?" I asked.

"Sure it is," Docker said. "Lazy old fox. Dogs damn near on him before he got outta there. Been too long since he's run. He already knows he's got old dogs back of him. Mad cause he's gotta run. Now he's got to teach those dogs. Ned's already droppin' back."

It was true, Ned's voice had drifted back from the leaders and had less volume.

"Colt's second and they're headed for Boar Hill," Yeager said.

"I know it," Docker said. "Be all right. Sally's no fool."

The dog's voices grew fainter, going away, then suddenly they were louder as the pack turned back toward us. Even with the stars and nearly a full moon it was dark out there, but I could make out the rise of a hill and the angle and the sounds of excited baying. There was a time of steady hounds on the trail, their voices rolling back to us, hitting the bottom of that dark ridge line and going up, you could hear their effort. Then a difference. One changing, mixing differently, moving up. Ned. A strained, eerie hound voice that made your neck hair tingle. Higher. Shrill.

Ned was clearly gaining on the other three dogs. It was a surprise to me and I looked over at Docker. His mouth had a set and I felt a jolt in my stomach.

"Henry!" Docker yelled.

Henry Yeager came forward and put his mouth to that steer's horn, blew for all he was worth, kept blowing, yet the voices out there didn't diminish.

Finally they began to subside, howls dwindled down. Yeager blew one more long one. Then it was quiet.

Docker roamed around like he'd lost something along the jumpy edge of the lighted area. I hadn't seen him like this, the flickering lantern setting off dark hollows in his face and big arms curved out, stomping in a strangely slow, bow-legged gait as if daring something to get in his way. Yeager just stared out at the night. There was a lot going on I didn't understand, didn't understand this situation at all, and surely I was confused looking out at the dark and hoping, really hoping that Ned and the other dogs would come in just like those dogs did before and everything would be all right. That's all I wanted right then, for those dogs to come in. I cursed myself for having any opinion about such a traditional thing as fox hunting, as if I knew anything about tradition. To me it was just foxes and dogs racing through the night in pursuit of some noble predator thing and maybe I had that all wrong too. I just came up with conclusions too quick. Foxhounds lived and died and hunted long before I'd come along to upset things.

A sound got our attention. All of us pressed forward except for Gary Bill back there against a tailgate, staring up at the stars.

Sally appeared out of the dark, tongue lolling, grinning, then Daisy. They ran between us and we patted and congratulated them while staring out at the shadows. Colt came in, worn out but happy, tail whipping to the beat of his head swaying back and forth.

We waited. I wouldn't look at Docker.

And then Ned came slow-loping in like the old warrior he was. Eyes blank in the light, skinny tail barely going, head low. I met him on my knees and he ran right into my arms. He just kind of collapsed into me and I held him up a little so nobody would think he was completely done. But he was. You could feel it in his shaky old muscles that just kind of let go.

"Get 'em in the truck," Docker said grimly.

Sally and Daisy jumped in the back and I lifted Ned, hoping no one would notice.

"Great night," Gary Bill said, loopy-like.

"C'mon," Docker commanded. "Get on in, Gary Bill."

"I'll ride in back," I said, and jumped in with the dogs before Docker could say anything.

We pulled out of the pasture and headed back down the rutty dirt road. In the lights from the other truck Yeager was hitching the wire around the gate, his dog Colt silhouetted in the front seat. Sally and Daisy were on me, bumping and licking and congratulating each other. It was as alive as I'd seen Daisy act, no whiny cowering now.

Ned wasn't looking so good. I got his head in my lap and kept stroking him and he kept emitting those soft groans that dogs will when they're very tired or content or both. But Ned's didn't have much breath in them. A limpness about him, in his eyes too. I held his head and kept stroking and talking to him real low, the way dogs like it when they're tired. Ned had a right to be shot, out of shape as he was, confined to a twenty-foot circle. He just needed more time to recoup than the younger dogs.

Ned started shaking in a different way, his whole body

quivering and jerking, foam coming out of his mouth, odd gagging noises. I just kept stroking his lean old body. I guess my tears mixed in with the foam as we bounced along. Daisy whined and nudged him a few times with her nose. Sally just frowned and looked away.

That night I carried Ned's body to the place Docker wanted him buried, out behind his house and the clothes-lines. The dirt was still warm from the day's heat till you got down to the sandy part. It wasn't bad digging except I knew I couldn't pause or look up. I dug the hole nearly to shovel-handle depth and placed Ned's cool body in it. Smoothed his floppy ears down and straightened his legs. Beyond wheez-ing and grunting directions, Docker didn't speak to me. This was for the best because my feelings were very confused that night.

Sitting on the edge of the cot and getting undressed I guess I must have stopped, because Gary Bill took a swipe at me with one of the hands he'd been waving at a fly.

"You done it, man," he said to me. "We'll be goin' home now. We're almost on our way."

I came half out of the fog and stared at Gary Bill. "What's that mean?"

"You killed his dog, man. It's done. We'll be out of here by the weekend."

Gary Bill was right.

We were packing our few clothes, my fishing reel and tackle in a separate brown paper bag.

"Janine's gonna be real glad to see me," Gary Bill said. "Bet she missed me plenty. Be goin' over to her house soon as we get home. I'll call and she'll sneak out. What you gonna do?"

I didn't know what to say. Home?

"Maybe," I began. "Maybe I'll try for one of those bass

in the cemetery pond." Gary Bill just chuckled and slapped down the lid on his suitcase.

Nice and cool on that Greyhound Bus headed back to the city, engine growling somewhere underneath us. Passing in the opposite direction the carnival headed into town, big trucks with Larson Brother's Fun Festival in fancy letters on the side, colorful animals and pictures of scary rides. Gary Bill was trying to engage a girl across the isle in conversation. I just slid deep into my own thoughts: Turner's Pond, that blue jay I killed for the straw, those people I'd met down there in Southern Missouri. Like anywhere you go, the people are the way they are.

But mainly I kept hearing the dogs. The rhythm of the whole hunt, all that baying bouncing together in the heavy air and coming back to us, rising on a hot trail to a pitch that made you want to get out there and run through the dark with them. I wasn't sure how I felt about everything that had happened, only that I had to keep thinking hard about it so I wouldn't ever lose the memory. It was the dogs I'd remember most, their grace in spite of meanness. I couldn't be mad thinking about the dogs.

And those tough little foxes.

WINTER COMETH

Paul Dirksen raised his eyes from *Wilderness Home; Essentials and Design*, and through the big cabin window scanned the brushy shoreline of his lake. Nothing beyond a few teal feeding along the reeds and that scruffy raven perched on the same snag, peering into the water. Every day he spent time on that branch protruding up from a sunken log. What the hell was he looking at? There was no food for an overgrown crow there. He can't swim or catch anything in the water. Stupid bird.

The lake brighter now, a mirror filled with spruce and clouds as finely etched as the originals. Bright rays sliced through cracks in the clouds to dry the clothes his wife had hung on frosty lines in the dim morning. She did not think it would rain or snow today, always optimistic, or maybe she only said it to get him to go out again. Go out there and do his duty. Be a man. How dare she!

He caught his deranged thoughts, beat them back, frowned

at the book's page.

"Do you think he will come today?"

Why must she ask again? "How could I know?" He realized his voice sounded a bit strained and adjusted, cleared his paper throat. "I think he probably will come because of the pies. He'll smell your pies all the way to Anchorage. The last time he nearly ate one by himself."

"Yes," she said, a soft smile. "He's a strapping young man, still filling out." She glanced at the back of her husband's head as she spread the plastic table cloth on the homemade table she had just wiped down with a warm, damp cloth. Steam curled from the tub on the wood stove. Soon the water would be hot enough for the boy's bath. She dipped the cloth in the tub and slowly rung it out, watching the water run down off her hands and wrists.

"I think he will come today," she said.

Her words caused Paul Dirksen to look up from the book he hadn't been reading to search the edge of the lake once again, along the line of trees where the trail from the edge of the muskeg led to his spruce log cabin. "It doesn't matter. I planned on going out anyway."

"I know," she said. "I'll fix you a snack when you're ready."

"I found a lot of sign yesterday. I know their routes now. It's simply a matter of timing."

"I'm sure you will be successful soon," she said gently. She busied herself with the wood fired oven, checking the pies. She rubbed her chapped hands, the way they were now, felt her eyes growing large and moist in the heat from the stove fire and took a deep, quiet breath, down on a knee gazing into the oven and thinking about how much food they had left.

"Tomorrow afternoon the car should be ready," he said. "I'll hitch into town and call the yard from George's Shop. He said it would be done and he'd put the bill in his drawer until I get back to work. I have a feeling the company may have been trying to reach me."

His wife didn't answer. She swung the cast iron door closed and rose, began washing the coffee pot and pumping in fresh water from the rainwater drum next to the counter. She put the heavy pot on the stove, next to the bath water the boys had hauled from the lake.

"Shall I send the boys in?" he asked, rising and placing the book on the chair.

"OK. Shoes off at the door."

Paul Dirksen paused at the top of the porch steps to watch his two sons and Bosco playing on the other side of the disordered clearing that was their yard. Boy's laughter exploded from frosty puffs punctuated with excited words while the black lab jumped and barked in the middle of the game.

Alaska homesteader. Certainly a term Paul never imagined would be applied to him. Yet it *was* him, and them, and the ruined career was his too, and the sadness in his wife's dark eyes when she thought no one was looking. He felt the heat, a blowtorch rising through his gut, cursed his weakness, feelings beyond his understanding that took control. He made his wife afraid, crazy, until she lashed out . . .

A sharp little crack, like a distant animal stepping on a dry branch. He listened, watching the boys. "Time to get in the house," he called.

"Hey, Dad," Paul Junior yelled, "that sounded like a shot."

"Might've been, season's open."

"Maybe it was Jim. Mom said he might come today."

Paul hoped it was Jim, even before his wife had said it. "Come on you little grub-butts, bath water is waiting."

"Ahh," Joshua moaned, shuffling toward the house, "I'm still clean from last time."

Paul Junior limped up the steps. "Are you going today?" he asked his father. "Can I go too? I'll be quiet. I'll carry stuff."

Paul smiled at his oldest son, felt a sense of pride and sadness. How could he do this to them? "Perhaps later in the season. There will be plenty of time to learn about hunting."

"Maybe Jim can teach me," Paul Junior said. "He knows everything. Mom said he'd come today."

"Maybe he will. Get in there now. Later you both get some of your mother's good pie."

They came reluctantly at first, yet began to hurry up the steps, Paul Junior favoring his damaged leg, past their father and open heavy plank door. "Shoes off," Paul said as they passed. Such beautiful boys, happy in this wild place so full of new adventures. Confident their father would take care of them. Keep them safe. Provide.

Another shot, no more than a pop. Paul Dirksen came down the rough-sawn steps and walked toward the trail heading around his lake. Bosco was ahead of him, trotting with ears cocked; he'd heard too. Paul followed the dog.

Jim holstered his K22 and walked over to pick up the second grouse. He'd wanted to take more, but the rest had flown off across the muskeg. This covey had been hunted enough to spook at a shot.

Halfway to the cabin he was greeted by Bosco, loping up with happy tongue flapping and going up on hind legs, planting his paws on Jim's chest and knocking him off balance till he was sitting on the mossy ground.

"Hey, Bosco, what's up? You're a little crazy today." He scratched the exuberant dog's back and head, taking a lick in the face. "What's-a matter? Bears around?"

The dog abruptly stopped and stared, black face ridged up, tail still going but a distant siren sound in his throat. Jim paused with his hand on the big head. "What'r you worried about? Here, check out these birds, you'll get some of the broth on your food."

The dog snuffled his big nose into brown feathers as Paul approached.

"Denise said you'd smell the pies all the way from Anchorage and be here today," Paul said, striding up to thrust out a hand as Jim was getting to his feet. Paul shook his hand vigorously, Jim a little uncomfortable, handshakes being uncommon in the woods.

"So how the hell are you?" Paul demanded. "What's it been? Over two months? You certainly look fit. I heard you were out on a job."

"Yeah," Jim was looking past Paul, then directly at the tall man, a rigid six feet plus, a man he admired. There was movement up the trail and he saw Denise approaching.

"I been in Clear a little over two months," Jim said. "Filling in for a field oiler that got hurt. They're still building that road, you know, not sure where the hell it goes, but we're building it. Good camp though. Put us up in a roadhouse with a bunkhouse built on the side. Bar right down the hall. Bar girls in there. None of 'em dancers though."

Paul grinned.

"I heard that," Denise said, walking up. "Aren't you a little young yet to be playing with bar girls? What is it now, nineteen? How come they even let you in?" She had the twinkle challenge in her eyes that always pinned Jim to whatever background he was standing against.

"Well . . . " Jim couldn't look at her directly, he'd thought of her too much and felt the shame. "See, in the Territory of Alaska they don't give you squat for years. They only want to know if you can do the work, pay for a drink and who do you know that got you on this job, and –" He cut it off, not wanting to talk about the camps, surely not the reason he drove all the way out here on his only day off. He just went to the camps to make some money and raise a couple or three after a ten hour shift. Always the youngest guy in camp he wouldn't get shit-faced with the rest, having found out where that could lead, the resentments. They knew he was there because his old man had some weight, which in reality meant he could never slack off or make a notable mistake.

"I didn't know if anyone would be here," Jim said. "The station wagon."

"Getting a new carburetor at George's," Paul replied, picking up the grouse by their scaly yellow feet, examining. A drop of blood fell off the beak of one bird. "Two shots, two grouse. Through the head as usual." He smiled at Jim.

"They let you get close," Jim said with a shrug. "My handgun's easy to shoot."

"Come on," Denise said, taking the birds from her husband. "Coffee's on and the boys bath water is ready and waiting for you two brutes to lift the tub off the stove."

They headed single file down the trail, Paul leading and Denise in the middle. She transferred the birds to her left hand and dropped back until she was at Jim's side on the narrow trail. He felt the heat rise in his face as she brushed against him, sending that sideways knowing smile. He couldn't help looking at her: ruddy cheeks, brows a little unkempt, that unattainable perfect mouth. Without makeup she was the most beautiful woman he'd ever met.

"We're all glad you made it today," Denise said. "I was afraid the snow would come and the road would be closed."

"It'll happen soon enough," Jim said.

"Yes." She looked away and pulled the wool shirt she wore like a jacket around her. "Another winter."

"Well, they'll clear it as soon as possible," Jim said, hearing winter depression already in her voice. "Anyways, you guys know what to do. How to deal with isolation. You've already done a winter and you all came out looking great."

She moved a little ahead, abruptly turned and forced a bright smile. "I want you to just relax and eat a lot of pie, OK? Can you stay over?"

"Have to be at work tomorrow morning," he said, and saw her smile become wistful. "Gregg called the afternoon I got back and said he needed me at the sporting goods store."

Paul stopped in the trail and faced them. "Now that you're back, have you heard anything about winter work in town?" As soon as he said it he knew he'd spoken too soon. "It's just that winter's coming –" Paul's jaw muscles rippled as he stared at the birds hanging from his wife's hand.

"I heard you got laid off," Jim said. "I'm campaigning. Don't worry."

"I appreciate your efforts, of course, but I know others also need winter work. Someone your father knows better perhaps who –"

"I said I wanted you in there," Jim said quickly. "It'll happen. Maybe pretty soon."

Cracks and leaks sprang in Paul's ridged composure, dulling his fierce blue eyes, drawing his chiseled face and stooping his square shoulders. Jim felt embarrassed for him, embarrassed and oddly ashamed of himself as the unqualified person this man had to depend on for a lousy warehouse job. But that's how it was these days, who you knew counted for more than what you knew. He didn't know if they were aware he'd heard the talk, that Paul had been one of the youngest captains in the Army, a brilliant career in the making. She'd stabbed him at the officer's club on the Fourth of July, they said. Helluva mess. Seeing them like this it didn't seem possible. Jim didn't want to know more or think about it. He just liked to be with them, admiring them for living out here in a log cabin in the wilderness. There weren't many people he admired, and in that way he thought it all right to think about how beautiful Denise was.

The two men lifted the heavy tub off the stove as the boys jumped around and yelled, daring one of the men to make a false move. They placed the tub in the center of the room and the boys stripped off the last of their clothes, danced around as if they were cold, though the cabin was warm with the stove going and the sun turning the lake to bright metal.

"What's the matter with your leg?" Jim asked Paul Junior.

"A bear bit it nearly off!" Paul Junior yelled, brows arched up and face stark. "Had to fight him with my pocket knife!"

Jim chuckled.

"He surprised a bear behind the woodpile a couple days ago," Denise said. "Fell and nearly broke his leg running for the house. Bosco managed to run it off. Paul was out hunting ..." Her voice trailed off.

"Bear forgot where he was," Paul said. "Coming into our yard like that."

Jim winced, glanced over and saw Denise watching him.

"Dad said he hoped you'd bring your rifle," Paul Junior said. "Me too!"

"I didn't say that exactly," Paul corrected, looking at Jim. "Only that if you did bring it you'd be welcome to do a little hunting."

Jim's mouth took a set against his screaming thoughts, *So exactly why didn't you bring your rifle? Why did you put it and the fresh handloads back in the closet?*

The men eased into two homemade chairs in front of the window. Denise brought steaming cups of strong coffee and they sat sipping and looking out across the lake. Jim liked drinking coffee Denise had made and soon felt better. Small fish were making a few dimples on the lake surface and Jim remembered Paul and Paul Junior telling about catching little Dollies in a nearby creek and hauling them in the station wagon up to the lake with water slopping out of the buckets. Joshua caught some too and they all worked a summer day driving back and forth from a creek that emptied into Goose Bay. Jim liked to see the fish eating bugs off the lake and thought he would help them next summer and they'd plant at least another two hundred. There were plenty of mosquitoes and other bugs on the lake and little fresh water shrimp the fish could eat in the winter. He considered bringing in some rainbows, but realized they weren't as well suited to surviving in this shallow lake for a winter. Dolly Varden were native, born to live under the ice.

"The otter still come?" Jim asked.

"Yes," Paul replied. "They were here a week ago. Four of them. I don't think they want our little fish, they just like to swim in the lake. It was opening weekend for moose and some fool hunter came in across the muskeg trail and took a shot at them with a high powered rifle. Had to run him out. What get's into some people?"

"The world's full of dangerous fools."

"Um." Paul lit his pipe. Smoke curled up spreading a burnt berries smell around the rough two-rooms-with-loft cabin.

The men sipped coffee and looked out at the lake.

Behind them Denise helped the boys finish their bath amidst laughter and complaints, Denise admonishing, the flurry of putting on clean clothes their mother had warmed next to the stove. "Hey, Mom, these pants are *wet*." "Stand next to the stove, they're barely damp." "Hey, Mom, these are Paul Junior's socks. I want *my* socks!" "Oh, all right . . . "

"I've been going out," Paul began, cleared his throat. "Marking the trails. There seems to be a lot of sign now. Mostly between Harold's Ridge and Three Lakes. Moose tracks."

Jim glanced at the older man. "The high country moose are moving down. Swampers moving up into the thick stuff. They know it's coming."

Jim added, "The big bears are moving too." When he entered the cabin he'd noticed a rifle against the wall near the ladder up to the boy's bunks and wondered why it wasn't near the door. Then he thought maybe Paul had finally bought a rifle. They had talked about it and he had urged Paul – not insisted certainly – that he acquire a rifle. One that fit his cheek like his best boots made his feet feel. A rifle he could bet his life on, all the while thinking, *How can you possibly be out here homesteading without even a rifle?* For all his knowledge of ordnance Paul had never hunted, but he'd found out what it was like to be treed by black bears while picking berries in their patch, treed by moose while walking their trails. Sitting up there in a skinny spruce scratched up from climbing fast, climbing for his life, wondering if his scratched blood smelled exciting. During the winter a wolverine had found their high cache and defecated on everything it couldn't eat or carry off. Another winter day when the family had driven the snow-packed road to town for supplies that overgrown weasel had returned and torn up both dogs and gotten into their cabin and destroyed whatever couldn't be eaten on the spot. This was a shock to Paul, how an animal could have such a mean attitude, as if it was personal. One of their dog's died of his wounds. Bosco still showed the scars.

Yet it ate at Jim that Paul still didn't really understand where he was. He'd brought his wife and kids out here to remake something, a desperate bid to reclaim a life, literally fighting the ground we all end up in, like a rebirth in fire and staring down the monster, except this was more about ice in the lungs and moving shadows which could at any moment become real monsters. You had to respect the harshness and those monsters so much you loved them because that was the only way to win. When Jim held it out he knew it didn't make sense, yet he knew it was true.

He heard the boys back near the stove, getting rowdy, finally Denise shushing them outside.

"So you have a rifle now?"

"Well, I might buy it," Paul said. "Harold brought it by. It's his spare rifle. He said I should try to get in some meat for the winter, which is certainly what I've been trying to do. He killed a moose last week, the day before the regular season opened. The afternoon before. He said he'd bring about a quarter of that by."

"And you're hunting. Learning the trails. How to move out there?"

"Yes," Paul said lightly. "I think I'm getting the hang of it. You just have to be patient."

"A cow," Denise said, joining the men by sitting cross legged on the floor between them with coffee cup balanced in her palm. "Harold shot a cow."

Jim looked from Denise to the black liquid in his cup.

"Of course that's illegal," Paul said quietly. "He even did it the day before it was legal to shoot any moose. But they don't seem to mind so much if you're, you know, people of the land. Homesteaders." The word caused Paul a moment's pause. "And you're expected to be discreet. Police up the area. Take care of things properly."

After a silence, Jim said, "Clarence Stockton came in the store yesterday. He took me to lunch." At Paul's questioning look, Jim said, "Clarence Stockton Guide Service. He's got a good rep, always booked. He let a guy go and offered me a job."

"Hey, that's great," Denise said. "It sounds like the break

you've been hoping for. So are you a guide now?"

"I have to let Clarence know by tomorrow morning. He's flying back to King Salmon Monday night and he wants me with him. Said he needs a guy to help on a grizzly hunt beginning Thursday."

"Sounds like a great opportunity," Denise said. "But you didn't say yes yet?"

"No." Jim realized they were waiting for him to explain. "It was kind of sudden. I wanted to get away and think about it."

"You came to the right place," Paul said. "We do a lot of that here."

It was good for a laugh. Denise topped up their cups and sat down again. The conversation slid into everyday things and Jim felt the lull creeping up. Being here with these people in this place a certain peace came over him.

After a pause in the conversation, Denise asked, "So do you want your pie now or after?"

"After what?" It was a rhetorical question, Jim knew.

"After you go hunting."

He saw the sympathy in her eyes. "I think later I'll be really hungry and enjoy it more. And I wouldn't want pie to weigh me down when I'm hunting."

"Well, no," Paul began, "don't think you're obligated in any way –"

"Does that thing shoot?" Jim asked casually.

"Well, I think so." Paul set his cup on the wood floor and went to get the rifle, held it out so Jim could take it. "Harold has sighted this rifle at a hundred yards and said it's good at that range."

Jim snapped the bolt back, released it out of the old Springfield, looked down the pitted barrel, replaced the bolt, examined the peep sight, the cut down stock, checked the stock length against his cheek; a little short, but he could compensate. It would be even shorter for Paul. An old military piece, trimmed some and worn thin. Jim sensed Paul over there, taut as a bowstring, straight nose pointing at him like an accusing finger. He wanted to be very careful right then.

"Cartridges?"

"Harold left these." Paul dropped four 30-06 cartridges in Jim's open hand. Jim looked at the cartridges, then up at Paul's hopeful expression.

"I had planned on getting more ammunition when I went to pick up the car tomorrow," Paul said.

"No problem." Jim gave a nod of reassurance. "I'll go see what I can find."

Paul was looking uncomfortable and started to speak, but Jim spoke first: "I was thinking about hunting last night and had my rifle out. Forgot it at the last minute. Anyway, it's late now, but maybe I can scout some, give you a heads-up for tomorrow."

They stood at the edge of the clearing. Jim checked the sky; scattered clouds hiding the sun momentarily, not much of a breeze. Bosco trembled at Jim's side.

"Take the dog if you want," Paul said.

No way would Jim ever want a dog along when hunting big animals. Yet this was different from a regular hunt and Bosco was different from most dogs. He was a homestead dog. And this weird hunt with a crappy rifle and econo crap ammo might be just the time to do something weird.

"I'll take Bosco," Jim said.

The forest closed around him. Jim sat on a moss-covered log and called the dog over. He admired the big beat up face, a black ear shredded, sore an extension of a scar at the edge of his left eye. He spoke quietly to Bosco as he examined each cartridge while loading the magazine. He carefully seated a cartridge in the chamber and levered on the safety.

"Four rounds and you never want to use your last one," Jim told the dog.

"We're going into the thick stuff. With the season open there won't be any young bulls eating water lilies this time of day. And we won't be taking a cow. We'll leave the cows for dumbshit Harold." Bosco stared at Jim's face. The dog's whole body looked full of electricity blurring his muscular outline.

Jim stood and shouldered the rifle. The dog stopped shaking. His eyes got that yellow cast. They were hunting now. Jim pointed toward a thicket of spruce and the dog angled off to flank.

After a few hundred yards Jim left the easy trail and moved into semi-darkness under old growth spruce, aspen and devil's club. Most hunters avoid the club and that was one reason Jim liked hunting it. He searched for the trails in there moose will sometimes use when they're on the move, trails that curve and turn with available browse and the hilly terrain, troughs in the ground worn by heavy animals. The site of a thousand pound bull moving quietly through heavy timber, wide antlers gliding like mist through mossy woods, that was a beautiful thing. There were lesser trails made by smaller animals and he knew moose may use these for a way when moving out of the high country and eating on the way. Black bears like it for the berry patches and grubs and critters underneath in the damp ground, and since club is a large leaf plant about chest high to a man it's good cover to hide their cubs. These black bears weren't acclimated to people then. They avoided grizzlies but weren't afraid of humans or dogs. Those that lived here in the deep woods weren't big bears, under three hundred pounds, heavier if they'd been into the salmon, but generally they were lean and quick.

There was sign of bears and moose right away, then a

fresh bear bed. The bed had some beaten down club, remains of berry plants and torn up moss and dirt, a shallow ditch to cool off in.

Bosco growled from a thicket and seconds later a yearling black bear went up a tree, scratch-scratch-scratch, and there he was fifty feet away, going up a tall spruce and glancing back with a snarl. Jim had the rifle out in front of him, looking for momma in that thick cover, but there was no other movement. Bosco appeared and they moved on.

A few minutes later a rustling next to the trail and a porky lumbered out, waddled a dozen yards and climbed into a bush. Jim paused a few feet away, watching the porcupine clinging unsteadily to a small branch too small for his weight.

"Good thing you have quills," he whispered.

He could hear Bosco moving off to his right, snorts, the rub of low bushes. The dog's pace was perfect and Jim knew they were both marking the other's position. The timber thinned a little, as did the cloud cover, and he moved around patches of sunshine penetrating like nervous theater spots.

Jim found a small animal trail and made pretty good time for a way, memorizing the ground ahead for several paces so he didn't have to look down so often, then on hands and knees to get under damp club and brush without making noise, dew brushing off on his cheeks, nose to nose with the beetles and feeling vulnerable, small, fear rushing through his veins, good animal fear, the tuning fork of survival. They knew how to use fear, get inside and pull fear around them like an alarm bell.

He came to a little opening, another trail crossing. He froze with his left hand in the air. The track he was about to place his hand in was a foot long and wide. Sunk deep in the soft ground. Grizzly. No more than a day ago, maybe less. He whispered over a shoulder and Bosco came in, sniffed the track, whined and backed up. They moved off on a different tack, passed out of the grassy spots and into dark timber again.

A squirrel chattered. Clicks of a raven's tongue. Beyond the raven Jim heard a branch brush something and swish back; maybe moose ahead. Jim stayed upright, moving even more carefully.

He began angling to get more separation from the dog, hoping if moose were near they might be confused with movement in two locations and turn his way. Jim moved as quietly as he could past fat wet stalks and over lumpy plush ground. Gusts through the tops of trees made dapples of bright light dance through the club, changing things constantly so you had to look hard to define shadows.

Jim stepped up on a moss-encased stump to get a better view. Balanced there with feet close together on the soft top of the stump. He couldn't see the ground anywhere beyond a dozen feet, but he noticed the breeze had shifted and flowed around his back, sending his scent in the direction he wanted to go. He wondered about moving in a different direction, judged the dog over there about sixty yards to his right, snuffling along. Stopped.

A grouse cooed. Breeze hushed through leaves.

Rummaging sound dead ahead where Jim faced.

Dog again, off to the right. Jim kept watching where the sound had come in front of him.

Right where he was watching a commotion – quick heavy feet hitting the ground, crashing brush, what appeared as a giant bowling ball rolling under the club, mowing a swath dead at Jim so fast he barely started to raise the rifle when the bear jumped up on a downed tree less than twenty feet away.

A mad black bear, head swinging, trying to pick up the

scent or sound that had brought it full speed. They were practically nose to nose, but it hadn't seen him yet. Jim didn't move a hair, not an eyelash. The head swung left and right, nose moving, left and right – swung far enough to block its vision behind a spruce trunk – in that bare second Jim snapped the rifle to his shoulder.

The head swung back and stopped with big black nose and glinty eyes directed right at Jim. He put the front bead on the pale patch in the middle of the bear's chest and squeezed the trigger.

At the blast the bear cart-wheeled off the log – the recoil upset Jim's balance and he went backward off the stump, came up on a knee with another cartridge in the chamber, ready.

Paul stopped splitting firewood and listened. The boys quit their game and looked from the woods to their father. Denise came out on the porch and stood near her husband. They listened.

"Was there only the one shot?"

"That's all I heard," Paul replied crisply. "He has his little twenty-two revolver to finish an animal. We may not have heard that." He turned to look at his wife. "He's a good shot. He has said it's a hunter's responsibility to shoot well so the animal doesn't suffer."

Denise shot him a look. "He doesn't even have his own rifle," she snapped. "Just that junk Harold dropped off hoping you'd be gullible enough to buy it." She cupped hands under her elbows and frowned at the trail Jim and Bosco had taken.

Paul felt heat rise behind his eyes. "Harold would never exaggerate about something that important. He is a homesteader after all."

Denise tore her eyes from the woods and stared at him. "Are you going?"

Paul hesitated. Then he mounted the steps, grabbed his holstered hatchet off a porch chair and threaded his belt through the leather so it hung at his side. On his other hip rested a sheathed knife, not the skinner but the big knife. He grabbed a coil of extra clothesline rope, clumped down the steps and marched across the yard.

"Be careful," she called, but he didn't look back.

Paul Junior caught up with him and begged to go along. Paul was ready to command the boy to stay but thought it would serve his wife right if he didn't. Paul nodded and continued on. Once inside the trees he stopped and looked down at his son.

"You will stay five paces behind me," Paul said, his voice deeper and sterner than he'd meant it to be. "And if I tell you to run, you will turn and high-tail it for the cabin. Understood?"

"Yes sir."

"You will not even look back. You will just run as fast as you can."

"Yes, Father."

Paul almost smiled. He's like me but better, Paul thought, thanks to his mother. He's better equipped for life thanks to her. Why did I let him come? He turned abruptly and they continued on the trail.

About a half mile in a sound caused Paul to halt and instinctively throw out an arm, as if Paul Junior would fall forward into whatever danger might be ahead. Bosco came galloping into view, tongue lolling happily, then Jim appeared, rifle hanging off his shoulder by the strap. Relief flooded into Paul's weathered cheeks and he went forward.

"We heard just the one shot . . . "

Jim stopped and smiled, looked at them both. "Hope you guys like bear stew," he said.

"All right!" Paul Junior said. "Let's go get it."

"Not you," Jim said. He spoke to Paul. "A big bear came through. Fresh track. Didn't dress the black, just bled it. We don't want any more scent than necessary till we can get it in. Paul Junior should go back right away."

Paul turned to his son. "Go now. Don't waste any time. Take Bosco."

Paul Junior started to say something, then yelled at Bosco and started running back over the trail. The dog soon overtook the boy and loped at his heels.

At the bear Jim shoved the rifle into Paul's hands and used Paul's big knife to quickly field dress the bear, pulling the entrails out and piling them on the yellow grass and soft moss the bear had fallen into. He rolled the carcass the other way to drain while Paul trimmed a small alder he'd cut down. Jim knelt next to the bear. He wiped his hands on moss and ran his fingers lightly over a rounded ear and down over the brownish muzzle. The rueful feeling came and he didn't push it aside, not today.

They hurried down the trail with the alder pole digging into their shoulders, the bear hanging by its tied feet over the pole. At the cabin they used the sturdy log fastened to trees that supported the boy's swing and hoisted the bear up with ropes tied just behind the clawed rear paws. Paul insisted on doing the skinning. Denise brought hot coffee and sat next to Jim. They watched Paul work the hide off the bear in one piece, black fur slowly reversing so the underside of the skin was exposed as Paul progressed.

Jim watched Paul and tried to just think about the hunt, but his thoughts were irreversibly slipping into the dark haunted place where a central part of his life plan kept going out of focus, a moving picture losing blurry composites. He didn't know what to do about this because there wasn't a contingency plan. Other interests and curiosities tasted like string today.

It wasn't about the hunt. Bear was coming for him and he'd done everything right. No suffering. Everyone happy. She was an average young female with dry teats and lots of berries in her stomach. Enough fat to eat well. Black bear was a bit coarser but as good as moose and just as high in protein. Harold had committed part of the cow moose and together it should be enough to get the family through the winter. All that was needed with good wild meat was a supply of beans and other vegetables and some canned fruit.

It was good here now, with good people. There was still time to decide the other thing.

"Now what's that frown about?" Denise said, pulling him back to the moment.

Jim shook his head. "Just thinking about Jimmy. We have the same name, but they call him Jimmy even though he's older. That school teacher down in Homer. You remember?"

"Yes," Denise said. "You said he was a guide."

"When bear season's on he is."

Jim saw Denise's questioning look and was sorry he'd even mentioned Jimmy. Yet who better to tell about it?

"Jimmy had a bad experience with a hunter last year," Jim said. "Two guys from Los Angeles. They surprised this old boar brownie on a kill. The bear stood up and this guy up and shoots him in the gut.

"The bastard gut-shot that grizzly," Jim continued quietly. "Then threw his rifle away and ran when the bear came. They both ran. Jimmy hung in there and stopped that bear an arm's length away. He went to his gunsmith after and had him re-barrel his 375 out to 450. That's what he carries now. They call it the 450 Watts. Said he needs the money. Has a child with special needs and teaching doesn't pay all that well."

Denise didn't say anything. For a few minutes they watched Paul working the skin off. The boys and Bosco were into another of the endless games they invented.

"Come on," Denise said. "Let's go for a walk," Denise smiled at his confusion and pulled him to his feet, hooked her arm in his and moved him along in the direction of the lake. Jim stumbled and tried to keep from bumping against her.

They stood looking at the rippled lake. Errant breezes danced across the surface in the sunshine. Above the trees a group of crows harassed an eagle.

"You really like this," Denise said. "Don't you."

"You guys picked a good spot. Some nice spruce along the shore over there. Solid ground where you put up the cabin. Got it up off the ground with a slot so the dog can get in away from the bears at night. You could use a decent power plant though. Even ten amps. Something to keep the radio going and emergency heat. You know, I've got a buddy that can get me stuff at the PX at a good price. I could pick one up and run it out next –"

She put a palm over his mouth. "You know Paul wouldn't feel right about that. He'll be back at work pretty soon. We'll be OK. Really."

Jim looked out at the lake. Mid-afternoon shadows crept out from the west shore. "It would just be a loan . . . "

"You aren't going to take that job, are you? The one you've been waiting for?"

It was a shock to hear her say it out loud.

"No," he said.

"Can you tell me why?"

"I feel bad about it," Jim said. "You know, Stockton's OK. Toby Tjionjon works for him, one the best there is."

"Good company for a young guy that wants to be a professional guide."

Jim took a breath, let it out. "It's too complicated to just say except I know I can't do that now. I wouldn't want to take somebody out there I didn't like. It would ruin it somehow."

After a while Denise pulled his head down and kissed his cheek. "Thanks for the bear," she said. "Now we'll go back and eat pie, James. And you will eat two big pieces or I'll feel slighted. And when you go back to town I don't want you to worry about us."

The rest of Jim's time at the Dirksen's was very pleasant. At Denise's insistence he had his two big pieces of wild blueberry pie with her strong coffee. Bosco took the last gooey piece of pie off his fingers and Paul Junior engaged him about hunting and rifles.

"Was it coming for you?" Paul Junior asked breathlessly.

"I don't know. Me or Bosco. I was in the way. She was doing the natural thing."

Paul smoked his pipe and talked about German craftsmanship and family philosophies. Denise flirted a little, just to tease a laugh out of him, and he thought she understood him better than anyone. He wondered if he'd ever meet another woman like Denise. A woman that knew when to call him James so it sounded right.

About a week later Paul was called into work and Jim thanked his father, did some extra work around his house. Paul worked a good part of the winter, except those times they were snowed in.

The Dirksens made a down payment on a lot in a development near Anchorage, and the following June they sold their homestead to somebody from "outside" and moved into the basement that had been formed on their new property. What would be the first floor acted as a roof, but they all seemed very happy to be there in that warm basement. The boys had a basket full of new interests. Jim thought Paul had lost some of his edge, the part that was good to lose, and Denise's smile lit up the room as if there were windows in those concrete walls and summer was streaming in. Her chestnut hair had a designed curl and she wore a medium shade of lipstick that changed her, as if the woman living on that homestead was simply a cousin to who she was now. Jim spent a few Sundays working with Paul on their new house, but being around them now changed a little more with each visit. Jim knew he would always be welcome in their home, but they were looking ahead now and he was a reminder of the past, an ordeal they had overcome.

Bosco didn't make the move to town. One afternoon Paul Jr. had lured his little brother out to pick the yellow rasberry-like cloud berries in a bog a hundred yards from the cabin, Paul Sr. had gone alone to check some rabbit snares he'd set, trying to learn the Indian method. Denise discovered they were not in the yard and began calling and almost at the same time heard the boys screaming. She ran in that direction and met them running toward her. They had surprised a bear at the bog and ran for home, a maneuver to a bear like waving a red flag at a bull. When the bear came Bosco held his ground, giving the boys time to get away. Paul told Jim he'd buried what was left of the dog out there on the trail behind the cabin. He'd sprinkled a pound of pepper in the grave and piled rocks on top.

That September, a few days before moose season opened, Jim drove his old Ford out to the deserted homestead and checked the spruce marker Paul had hammered down into the perma. The marker was still there and the stones over the shallow grave were in place. He found a few more heavy stones and stacked them on the grave.

On the way back Jim took the path around the front of the empty cabin and looked up at the dark reflection in the front window. A squirrel scolded from under an eve. There were triangular cobwebs in the window corners. An X-frame used for cutting firewood stood in front of the cabin and Jim wondered absently who had moved it out here from where it belonged near the woodpile

He sat on a mossy stump in front of the cabin for a while drinking coffee from his thermos and watching trout make dimples on the surface of the lake. He wondered if they could reproduce in this little lake and if the otters would come back and eat some of them.

A raven glided along the shore and pumped it's wings to land on a snag sticking out of the water. Jim remembered seeing the bird when Paul and he had sat looking out at the lake.

"You have your favorite place, " Jim said. "And for a little while this stump will be mine."

Short Story

"Every season some character's screw up makes the paper," David Hammersfeldt said loud enough to carry into the kitchen where his wife was preparing dinner. "Are they so desperate for news they have to quote some imbecile who can't tell a buck from a doe?"

"Bucks and Does, dear?" Elaine called back. "The bowling teams?"

"No," David said louder. "I mean the ones with real horns on top of their heads where God put them so any fool could tell what he was shooting at."

Elaine's flaxen-streaked hair and tanned face angled into the kitchen archway. "Not everyone has the David Hammersfeldt laser eye. Dinner in twenty minutes? I'm just going to warm up those barbecued ribs from Sunday with fresh asparagus."

"Could we make it forty? The kids are always late anyway."

"Not tonight," a little impatience in her voice, "Rachel has loads of homework and Robby has to get back to school for X's and O's. You know how Coach is about punctuality. Sometimes I think you two are related." She disappeared back into the spacious kitchen.

"I like Randle, he's a good coach. Certainly Rob could use some extra practice in punctuality."

"Couldn't we all," she shot back, out of sight. "He must get it from me."

David heard the tone and didn't reply. He settled back in the recliner, the satisfying squeak of fine leather, feet on matching hassock, a king in his castle, raised the crystal glass and tasted single malt scotch; his medicine for a day to keep the beast at bay. Perhaps it had been one of those days for Elaine too. He decided to have another scotch, dropping in one ice cube made with filtered water.

Earlier, he'd nearly fired a good employee over a dumb mistake on a remodel. When his secretary, good-ol'-easy-going-plug-away Susan, had suggested it was just that old full moon again, he had an urge to send her there. That's when he rushed out with barely a word and gunned his pickup out of the parking lot. At least he knew enough to leave before becoming completely anal.

Most days he loved building custom homes and remodels from the concept an owner would struggle to explain. He could present a plan that caused excitement to jump in their eyes and it always gave him a private rush. But later the good feeling was inevitably diluted by extra costs incurred with their infernal whims. Still, it was the work he had chosen, and there were a lot more good days than bad. He wasn't the cheapest contractor in town, yet he normally had work six months ahead. Of course this cycle of low-rate home loans couldn't last forever. Materials going up faster than inflation . . .

Shutup, he told himself, and had another sip, sloshed the smoky burn around while considering the story in the local section about some fool shooting a doe when he thought it was a buck. A responsible hunter would simply have admitted his mistake and paid the fine instead of whining his fool's story to some reporter. Just pay the bill.

David considered a cigar. Elaine thought cigars a health hazard. Yet an occasional cigar out on the patio surely seemed reasonable. Why can't a man have a cigar now and then? He looked over at Rollo and was met by two loving brown eyes. The Brittany tensed and curled an excited lip under his gaze.

"I know," David said quietly, "I've neglected our covenant lately."

Rollo rose, cautiously inched toward him. "Guess I came home like a blind pig," he said, extending a hand. The dog laid a tan-freckled muzzle on his leg. David began scratching behind an ear and Rollo groaned appreciation. "How about the white ear now?"

Elaine's head appeared in the kitchen archway. "You promised to take Rollo hunting after work this week." Her tone made it a reprimand.

"I know," David said a little sharply. Sometimes his wife's ability to read his thoughts caught him of guard, made him feel vulnerable. Well why wouldn't he be that way with Elaine? Of course he was. He thought of the amazing day they met, bringing the image up like an evocation. He was still crazy then and her voice had cut through his brain like an electric current. After seventeen years the juice still hummed and crackled between them.

"It *is* Thursday," she added. "That poor dog feels more neglected than I do lately."

David's thoughts were jerked back to the present and his eyes snapped toward the kitchen arch, but no one was there. "What does that mean!" he demanded. "What am I being accused of now?"

Elaine reappeared in the archway and struck a provocative pose. She was still trim and had a way of setting her lovely mouth that inevitably ruined whatever aggression he happened to be entertaining, and he realized she was just trying to jolt him out of his foul mood.

"Why nothing, dear," she purred, and twirled away.

David settled back in the chair. "I want you to know," he yelled at the archway, "that it is *usually* a pleasure to be married to someone smarter than me."

"Oh, you can do better than that," she called.

David smiled.

She leaned around the archway again. "Rollo is now taking the neighbor dogs hunting up on the ridge. They show up on the patio every morning and he leads them out through the sage like a safari bound for dog nirvana. And up they go. Most give it up halfway to the ridge, a few last almost to the top, but Rollo doesn't care. He's hunting and flushing birds."

"What's he getting up? Pheasants?"

"Pheasants and chukars. There are lots of chukars on the ridge lately."

"Really? Chukars?"

"Yes," his wife confirmed. "Twice that dog has come back with feathers stuck to his muzzle. That's how desperate he's become. We're all so desperate," she added with a theatrical hand describing an arc in the air, causing David to chuckle as she again disappeared into the kitchen.

Then he frowned and wondered if he *had* been a bit distant lately. When was the last time he'd taken Elaine to dinner? Of course this was a busy time for both of them. So what? That's when you should make time to do something special for her.

Of the game birds David hunted with Rollo, chukars were Elaine's favorite table fare. He liked them too, but more for their speed and the difficulty the dog had in holding them for the flush. They were natural mountain birds with the odd trait of running uphill and flying down, so it was difficult for dog and hunter. Rollo was a little small for a Brittany, though plenty sturdy with straight legs and loads of endurance.

David no longer cared much for hunting, but with Rollo it was always a pleasure, the two of them slowly walking an early field, larks and other birds talking up the new day, brush and fence lines glistening with dew in frosty slanting light. It had always been the hunting, not the killing. Just being alone in open country with your dog.

Around the house he couldn't compete with the kids who were far more demonstrative in their love for Rollo than he could ever exhibit. The kids made him see his walls from a new angle, causing him to track back to how they had been erected in his early life. How could Elaine have loved him then? He picked a stray hair off the dog's nose. Hunting season was half over and they'd only been out twice. The weather, he'd said when Elaine brought it up, too warm, too many crops still up. Need a cold snap.

There had been frost every morning for a week.

David took another sip of scotch and closed his eyes, let the back of his head relax into soft leather, thought about the box of excellent cigars in the garage given by a grateful client. He could get a cigar and another scotch and sit out on the patio. Or he could get off his ass and do something.

Abruptly he sat up. Rollo's ears flapped back, brown

eyes wide, head steady. David went to the window, studied the mountainous horizon ignited by the descending sun.

Rollo's stub of a tail began scrubbing the carpet. David strode quickly into the bedroom with the dog trotting in his footsteps. From the gun cabinet he selected his favorite, a vintage Ithaca 20 gauge over and under. He grabbed the appropriate shell belt out of a cabinet drawer, slung it over a shoulder and marched through the kitchen. David looked back at his surprised wife.

"A backyard hunt is better than nothing," he announced, sliding the patio door open.

"OK, but shouldn't you take your brush coat and boots?"

He looked down at his sneakers. "No time, the light is nearly gone." As if to confirm his words, Rollo uttered a low howl.

"Here." She grabbed his flannel lounging shirt off a hook next to the garage entry and threw it to him. "Do watch your step. And be careful, Rollo is our only dog."

Following too quickly behind excited Rollo, up the steep trail toward the top of the ridge through strong-smelling sage and high yellow grass, David became winded. He called the dog and paused, rested part of his weight on the shotgun and looked back at the tops of his neighbor's houses, beyond to the great valley where the town spread out in a patchwork of building dots and winking lights marked by the curve of the river. A community a little bereft in the culture department perhaps, but long in basic values. Elaine had loved the town at first sight and agreed basic values was culture enough. He'd brought his young pregnant wife here when they had little more than their clothes and a few pieces of furniture.

He was part of the landscape now, a local businessman who paid his bills and supported community activities.

Accepted. "Only a concept," he whispered. But one he savored when it was just Rollo and he together. In those private moments he could stand aside and see his identity, where he'd been and what he had become, and it caused a chill to run up his spine from the fear his present life was more than he deserved.

Rollo made a sound and David slid slowly, lazily, down the length of the shotgun until he was sitting on the ground. The dog wallowed in his lap amid snorts and urgent whines.

"I know," David said. "So what have you been finding up here? I hope you haven't run all the birds off with your relentless pressure." He loaded the shotgun.

They made their way further up the ridge through good cover with clover and bunch grass around the sage, shafts of wild wheat overripe and drooping. The dog was into scent everywhere, snuffling along but moving carefully, a signal there could be game close by. Suddenly a ringneck pheasant thundered up well out of range, orange and white colors flashing in the last rays of the sun. The dog started, then looked back.

"Don't ask me," David said. "I don't know why he got up way out there. Unless you've been hunting him too hard. Go find another one."

Rollo assumed a serious look and moved ahead. Soon he was into more scent and began crisscrossing slowly, trying to locate the bird.

The final rays spiked above the mountains. Another twenty minutes and they would have to head back.

Under the sage were dark shadows and the dog moved in and out of them, letting his nose lead the way. It had cooled and David was glad Elaine had tossed him the extra shirt. He thought of her order to be careful. There were rattlers in the area and he wondered if they might come out at this time. Hunting dogs were lost every year to rattlesnakes, their noses down where they were most likely to get struck in the face.

They hunted through a shallow draw and up over the next rise.

Suddenly Rollo froze, then began to slink forward, head steady. David followed with the gun partly raised in anticipation of a preemptive flush.

The dog went on point, ridged from muzzle to straight stubby tail. David paused to admire Rollo. Then moved in.

The bird exploded up out of a thicket of yellow grass, a black silhouette against the dark orange sunset, fat and short-tailed, a chukar that would most certainly make Elaine happy. David swung smoothly on the bird as it peeled off down the hillside and at the blast of the 20 gauge the bird toppled in a puff of feathers.

"Get him!" David commanded, but Rollo had marked and was already crashing through sage. Tail quivering at maximum rpm, Rollo brought the bird in and David reached down and took it from the dog's gentle mouth.

And then David realized he had just shot a hen pheasant. A hen pheasant without the usual long tail feathers. He examined the bird and realized the feathers had been removed, ripped out.

David looked at Rollo who was very happy. He blinked at the illegal hen pheasant. David gazed out at the darkening sky over his town, then furtively looked around to see if anyone had witnessed his heinous act.

Below, a neighbor was doing something in the back yard. Though the man was several hundred yards away and it was nearly dark, David hunkered down with the bird. He shushed the dog and sulked there in shadow. David realized he was trembling. He put an arm around the dog and spoke quietly. Rollo became uneasy, whined, but David held on.

"Stay," he whispered. "Please."

Finally the man below disappeared into his house.

David unloaded his shotgun and gripped it and the bird's feet in one hand so he could push coarse sage limbs out of the way as he moved in a crouch down the ridge. He stumbled and fell into a dark pocket, limbs raked his face. Rollo wanted to race ahead, but David whispered urgent admonishments, forcing the dog to stay with him.

At the edge of their property where clipped grass began, David stopped to examine the open area between him and the patio door. He could see the dining room lights were on. Again he told the whining dog to be quiet and put a controlling arm around him. There were lights on in the neighbors houses. Through a window he watched the Duncan's sitting around the dinner table eating, talking.

When David was sure no one was in adjoining backyards he released the dog and they made a dash for it. At the patio door he composed himself, walked in like a relaxed hunter coming home from the field, which, he told himself, was true. It was a joke really, accidentally killing an illegal bird, nothing to be very upset about. He was home now. An accident.

David stopped just inside the door. His family were busily clearing the table after dinner. Robby already had his letter-jacket on, ready to leave for the team meeting.

"I'm a game law violator," David blurted and held the bird out like an offering.

Elaine froze and stared at him. Robby and Rachel did not notice their father's strange tone or expression or their mother's suddenly intent look and immediately pounced on this opportunity.

"Don't worry, Dad," Robby said in an exaggerated whisper, "I won't rat you out to the game warden. Even though he's Kevin's dad."

"The tail you see . . . I didn't leave it out there. I'll take care of it properly."

"Sure," Robby said, pushing long, green-streaked hair away from his eyes. "But I don't know if we should help you eat it. Wouldn't that make us accessories or co-conspirators or something?"

"Yeah, Dad," Rachel added. "Do you want us to go to prison?" She showed him her mother's mischievous grin.

"An interesting thought," he replied. "It might adjust your sense of values."

"*Da-ad.*" Rachel edged away, frowning now while watching her father's face.

"The dog did it," Elaine said with strained cheerfulness. "He disguised that poor bird as a chukar. I guess Rollo should go to the slammer."

David stared at her. He looked down at Rollo. "C'mon, butt-biter" he said. "You can help with the butchering." The dog eagerly followed him out to the attached garage.

David gutted and skinned the pheasant under the light over the utility tub. He put the carcass on the edge of the tub, rinsed his hands thoroughly, tied the plastic bag of guts and feathers shut. The pheasant carcass looked small on the edge of the tub. He moved away from the light and sat on a picnic bench that had been brought in for the winter. The dog sat in front of him and whined softly. David seemed not to notice.

Elaine entered the garage. She sat on the bench next to him. "Your dinner's in the oven," she said. "It may be a little dry."

"It will be more than adequate for a criminal."

"David, please. It was an honest mistake."

He shook his head. "The silhouettes are different, even without the tail feathers. The wings. Flight pattern. I should have been paying better attention." He got up and began washing the bird again.

"Like the man who shot the doe?" Elaine said. "I read the article while you were up on the ridge. Did you read the whole thing?"

"No," he admitted.

"He really didn't come across as making excuses. There was a branch over the deer's head and he thought they were horns. He sounded very apologetic. I just wondered if you'd read that part."

David turned, the dripping carcass in his hand.

"You thought you were bagging a chukar for me, didn't you?"

He nodded.

"Then let's call it one," she said. "Let's eat it together tomorrow night with a wild rice mix and that bottle of merlot we've been saving. Tomorrow is Friday and the kids have commitments. They won't be home until late."

"Elaine, I was scared up there."

She squeezed her eyes shut, squeezed them so tight moisture ran down her cheeks. She blinked finally and looked around the garage.

"Those times are over, David. It was another life." She suddenly shook her head, tousling hair, glared at him.

"*It was a tiny little mistake.* They don't put people in prison for shooting a pheasant!"

"I know." His frown cut gray creases in his face. "But.. . I just wanted to get home to you and the kids."

Elaine rose and came to him, put her arms around his waist and pressed her head on his chest. "Don't," she whispered. "Nothing happened. Let it go." Rollo whined and wedged himself between their legs.

The bird carcass fell into the utility tub and he enclosed his wife in his arms. She fit perfectly there. He would let it go as she asked, because he could refuse her nothing. They would eat the bird and drink the wine and she would tell the kids to be quiet about this.

No one would find out.

THE DYNAMIC DUO OF HIDDEN COVE ROAD

You could say it was mainly Mom's and my little brother's fault we ended up with Poncho. They went to look at pups one day and came back with two brothers, Kooky and Poncho, which even as pups looked and acted nothing alike. The mother was Pomeranian and French Spaniel, whatever that is, and they thought the father might be border collie and something else, although nobody could be sure. It may have been this ambivalence regarding roots that gave Poncho his personality, which was very different from his woosie brother's.

Poncho was not beautiful. Nor was he a great hunter in the classic sense, or any good sense really. He lacked discretion and discipline in the structured pursuit of game, although he did guard the chicken house and during his last two years he guarded Dudley. Poncho stalked and chased everything madly, especially UPS trucks, which is why he had only one eye. The good eye, the bluish one opposite the scarred, whitish, marbled thing, tried to compensate for the loss by bulging to hideous proportions at anything that got his attention. He also smelled like an open sewer, a peculiar trait impervious to serious bathing, disinfecting, herbal shampoos and ion treatments. Dad thought the stench could be the result of mange, which was perennial on Poncho's squat, elongated, pig-like body.

Yet lady dogs, those in romantic moods, coming into their time of excitement, found Poncho irresistible. And Poncho knew this as surely as a diviner knows where to bore a well. His swinish nostrils would flare, testing the air, and off he'd go in search of another victim that couldn't help succumbing to his charms. It was my theory Poncho brought out the covert, destructive side of those girl dog's inner confusion.

Dad called Poncho's allure one of the mysteries of nature and tried to contain him. Stoutly fenced in, Poncho dug his way out. Locked in the garage, Poncho chewed through the solid fir door. Of course Mom wouldn't allow him to be corralled in the house, and I thanked her for that.

Some of our neighbors became distant, even unfriendly. Even those of us family members that agreed in principal to what the growing mob thought should be done with Poncho were sometimes shunned in public. There were a lot of ugly, smelly pups around.

One Sunday morning I was coming into the living room from the kitchen when a loud pounding on the front door startled Dad as he was reading the paper. He put the open paper down and, eyes darty, arms curved tensely away from his body, slowly rose from the couch. We looked at each other questioningly, but we already had our suspicions. I followed him to the front door. He turned to me.

"Better stand back, Fay," he said.

When Dad opened the door Carl Swanson, a neighbor from up the road, rushed in, causing us both to jump back.

"Arthur, *the creature came back!* I'm sure he actually accomplished the travesty this time. *You promised!*"

"Now, now," Dad said in his patient voice. "I'm sure it isn't all –"

"The fiend came right through the fence! Chewed and clawed his way in like some cave animal! Good God, Arthur, he mounted her right there in the front yard, drove her poor little nose into the grass . . . Susan's mother visiting from Minneapolis." Carl slumped against the wall.

"Well, Carl, they are dogs you know. They have their special times when –"

"*Dog?*" Carl straightened, eyes wild. "No, no, my Cleo is a dog. That creature of yours is *something else*. Do you realize what this means? Can you *imagine* the pups? The *smell*?"

Dad cleared his throat. "Perhaps, Carl, you would like to come into the living room and have some coffee. Or nice homemade wine?"

This seemed like *deja vu* to me, just more pain I guess for Dad, who had built the Swanson's house. They didn't know when they bought it there would be a Poncho in their future. But hey, he kept the coons out of their flower beds. He murdered a opossum and left it on their doorstep – or someone else's – every week that he wasn't busy being romantically involved. You can't expect one weird little dog to be like everything. And regarding his hunting expertise, some of the neighbors appreciated the thinning of destructive animals and made him special treats. Poncho visited them on specific days each week. In fact, his hunting range had become so large that he was sometimes out overnight. There were actually people that put burlap and old blankets they were going to throw out anyway out on the porch for him to sleep on. No one, of course, liked him enough to allow him inside their house. Our neighbors are clean, decent people.

The glitch was, Poncho was my little brother Marvel's dog, so Dad couldn't just end the problem with his shotgun, although he threatened to often enough.

But about the time it couldn't get any worse, it did. And it all happened in such an innocent, heroic way nobody could have suspected how it would work out. You could say it started when Dad finally decided to chain Poncho. "Stake him out," was how he put it. "And may the coyotes take him out of our misery." Since we lived on an island in Puget Sound I was pretty sure we didn't have any coyotes, but Dad said he'd seen one near the bridge. I suggested it may have come across as a displaced resident of the wild animal farm near Sequim, but Dad remained convinced we had a gang of coyotes and they, along with the raccoons, were after his chickens.

But what happened was that Marvel (his given name Marvin), a boy who found true happiness wallowing in the excremental mosaic of the animal kingdom, was on the beach near our house one morning and saved a duckling from being the certain breakfast of a black Lab who lived nearby. The Lab was determined to make a meal of the duck, but Marvel was even more determined it wouldn't, and the struggle came down to Marvel holding a piece of raised driftwood and standing his ground between duck and dog.

Marvel brought the duckling home and for three weeks it slept in the folds of an old shirt right next to Poncho's bed at the foot of Marvel's bed. Yes, Poncho had been allowed in at my brother's insistence, because the duck liked him. Of course no one wanted to venture into the wasteland of his room anyway, so it wasn't like we had to give up any territory. Poncho and the duck formed a bond. In hindsight, you could say we should have seen an ominous pattern forming, but it was just a duck after all. It wasn't even one of the colorful wild ducks we had a multitude of, but a basic white, uninspiring, domestic duck somebody had dumped on the beach. Marvel named it Dudley.

For a couple of weeks it swam in Poncho's water dish, until the dog led Dudley down to the small stream and pond in back of the house. Poncho would stand in the shallow pond and the duck would swim back and forth between his legs and splash water at the dog's face. Dog and duck began going on walks together in the woods. They took sun naps together on the front porch, Dudley's long neck draped over Poncho's fetid one. They ate side by side. When Poncho barked, Dudley quaked and flapped his wings. The duck seemed to be acquiring canine traits, and growing large very quickly.

"I do not see any good coming of this," Dad warned. "The dog is warping the duck into his own image. It could be one of the mysteries of nature. We should consider eating the duck soon. Before it gets any bigger and stranger."

My brother's stricken look stopped Dad for the time being.

Poncho started Dudley off on squirrels. Poncho would chase a squirrel with Dudley flapping and squawking along in his wake until the rodent was treed. Dudley would then fly, wings beating madly and with great effort, being already an obese white duck, up to the level of the squirrel in the tree and sort of zero in on the terrified animal, causing it to leap into another tree or into space - and often right down into Poncho's waiting jaws.

As if this disgusting behavior weren't enough, the duck took a dislike to me and would attack my bare legs whenever

I wore shorts, even if I was with a date, its beak like snapping pliers. I told Marvel if Dad couldn't do the deed I'd snap its skinny neck like a pretzel and take it back to the Lab that lived a few doors down. But Marvel went screaming to Dad who caved like I knew he would.

The two creatures expanded their efforts to include raccoons, opossums and even ringneck pheasants, of which the island had quite a few, and for all their cunning these savvy, coveted birds were cajoled somehow by the duck's abrasive calling to come within range of Poncho's eager jaws. Dad suspected Poncho had introduced the duck to pheasant flesh; this Marvel refused to accept and I did not even wish to contemplate. Mother sided with Dad. They insisted something would have to be done.

But quick as you can say Dad got out his shotgun, Poncho and Dudley changed tactics. They no longer stalked wild game. Poncho introduced the duck to spinning tires.

They say there's a lot to life that doesn't make sense, and maybe shouldn't, but you have to wonder about a stinking one-eyed dog and a crazed oversized white duck which had it made in the usual ways and chose to be obsessed by spinning tires on moving vehicles, especially brown ones. This does not match up with the pragmatic sense one tends to apply to the animal kingdom.

Not that they weren't good at it.

One day, when I slipped out our drive to the road to wait for my date – he was a nice boy really, usually, but Dad didn't like his long ratty hair and bead necklace which included a few human teeth.

There isn't much traffic on our road. Wide ditches on each side of the blacktop fill up in summer with dandelions and tall, yellow grass that sways in the breeze and the wake of passing vehicles.

The sound of a distant motor. I looked down the road, then watched with some trepidation as a large white duck head periscoped up out of the grass, looked around. Mutterings from the beak. A chewed charcoal nose floated, twitching, up out of the grass, a bulging eye. The vehicle came into view, brown, boxy. A UPS truck, the favored quarry. The brown nose and bulging eye sank down out of sight, the muttering duck head lowered so only its beady eyes were above the blossoming grass. The truck rumbled slowly closer as the driver leaned out to see names on mailboxes. Suddenly the two creatures exploded out of the ditch, one by ground, the other by air. The one by ground snarled viciously and tried to bite through six ply tires while the heavily airborne creature hit the windshield and slid around until it was inside the cab, attacking the driver.

There were some sharp wheel moves before the truck swerved into the ditch and thumped to a stop at an odd angle. The shaken driver stumbled out of the dust. He grabbed up rocks and started throwing them at the creatures that had attacked him, but they were already nearly out of range, gleefully barking and quaking.

I began running then, my t-shirt riding up and sandals flapping, but I was too late to save Mooch – my date's nickname, his actual name being Randy – and watched in horror as duck and dog ambushed him just as he was turning onto our road. Unfortunately the driver's window was down. Dudley gave him a beak slash across the forehead and Mooch followed the example of the UPS driver.

This was Game Perfect for Poncho and Dudley. Never mind the raging neighbors they practiced on to perfect their craft, the banged-up cars and nervous episodes they induced from our erstwhile friends and supporters. There were threats against Dad and a petition went around aimed to excommunicate us from the church for not slaughtering the dog and duck in question. Never mind my lacerated legs or Marvel's pleadings or the tire remnants strewn around our yard, it was all simply a means to an end for Poncho and Dudley to reach their pinnacle of effectively cutting off UPS service to our end of the island.

"We can no longer come to Hidden Cove," the letter from UPS said that was sent to everyone in our community. "It's become an insurance requirement. Your neighborhood has been designated unusually hazardous. You can pick up your packages at the hardware store in town."

Of course the community fought it and UPS, being sensitive to public scrutiny, had to resume service. But what they did, we soon found out, was bring a driver over from Walla Walla in eastern Washington where the prison is, and in fact he had actually worked at the prison communication center before being hired by UPS. Not that everyone shouldn't be given a chance to move laterally or whatever, but with his prison experience he may have had an unfair advantage in the Poncho-Dudley game. Some even said there was a bounty involved.

The thing was, Poncho and Dudley only had to lose once seriously, and they did one rainy fall day the very first time this new driver took the route. They went out under the wheels they loved. It was a grisly mess and Dad, in a move meant to soothe Marvel's grief, threatened to shoot the driver, and did in fact dent the truck's brown flank with a hefty rock.

Marvel was the only one who cried at dog's and duck's passing, but a month later Dad gave him a baby short-eared goat. That goat grew up hooked on shoelaces and tulip bulbs. Tulips are my mother's favorite flowers. At least I had the sense to quit wearing shoes with laces.

DIFFERENT PARTS OF A CLAIM

Felt just like a year ago, headed south on I-55 again except a different dog in the back. Not kenneled in the pickup bed, mind you, but right behind us on the little bench seat in almost the same setup as back then.

I had to wonder about Big Jake's state of mind. As a professional he knew you did not change any mode on a dog – 'specially an unseasoned pup – when you were already changing locations and doing the necessary things to get ready for the Southern Trials. True, Lady L was an exceptional pup. Special in ways that give a trainer those little electric currents in the belly and cause him to stare off into space like some day-dreamin' corn picker. But it seemed to me Jake was putting undo hardship on Lady L by having her ride up front when she'd never done it and wasn't comfortable with it. Bonnie on the tape player notwithstanding, I hoped my silence would cause him to think about what he was setting this little dog up for.

"About here we started getting snowflakes last year,"

Jake said. "Remember? In that damn Rambler with Honey kenneled in the back seat space. Nothing but snow and ice."

"Like it was yesterday's nightmare," I replied.

"Taking her to make love to Dr. I-J was about like taking Helen back from that Trojan guy. It's a wonder she had any heat left by the time we got to Lou-siana. We put her through hell that night."

"Not to mention ourselves," I said.

Jake didn't notice the sarcasm, his mind being situated in the present future and Lady's ultimate potential. But for sure I remembered being a little north of this same stretch of highway when the sound of a rod knock was about enough to knock you out of the seat.

"Can't be," Jake said then. "Brand new F-150. Only used it as a demo. Can't lose a damn rod in 5,000 miles."

"Does sound like a classic case," I said, trying not to sound too grim.

Jake pulled onto the shoulder. Raised the hood and checked the oil. Looked over the clean new engine. Slammed the hood down. Got in and slammed the door. Sat there for a time and I did check to see if there was steam coming out of his ears.

Finally he said, "Guess we better go back and get the Rambler. And I may kill that twit at the car store."

We drove slowly back to Beltsville, expecting at any moment the increasing rod knock to end with a grating-seizure sound and the rear wheels to lock up. But that malignant engine lasted long enough for us to limp home where we tore the rear seat out of Jake's Rambler, kenneled Honey back there and set off again, having lost about eight hours and now well into night and Jake driving 80, right into the worst ice storm they'd had in southern Missouri in about 40 years. There was a timeliness issue regarding Honey's physical readiness and her big date down south with the one and only Dr. I-J – certainly a great English setter sire in the traditional sense – a date Jake had put a great deal of importance on and he was determined to see it, well, completed productively. Honey seemed equally ready to tackle any obstacle in the interests of completion and I wondered at that time if he'd talked to her, as a trainer will, especially to a favorite, regarding her upcoming date. Jake had referred to it more than once as a Date with Destiny. Destiny's form was sure one of the prettiest, most pampered and indulged sires in American English Setter history, but in his case maybe it wasn't exaggerated. Honey was a fine dog in so many ways and what she lacked Dr. I-J had, so there was sound logic as well as practical hope in this match, so maybe you could accuse me of being a little jaded for having doubts. But I wasn't jaded about Jake, and I did want this plan to go well and for him to end up with the kind of pups most trainers only see in their dreams. Except you know what they say about dreams and the best laid plans.

So that night when we drove from a cold rain into the teeth of the worst ice storm I ever want to see, my doubts were growing by the minute as the sleet began to clog the Rambler's wipers, the highway became a series of glaring emergency lights and we slithered past huddled groups along the road standing next to tangled wreckage.

All the motels were full; I mean places you wouldn't stay in if you didn't have the money for a room. Motels got filled that night that hadn't had a good payday since the flood of '83 and should have been swept away in those muddy waters. And the ice kept on down there past Missouri's boot the Arkys still claim should rightfully be theirs. Around Memphis ice-incased branches fell across the road and we drove over some of them. Right in front of us a semi slid off and wedged sideways in a wide ditch. We would have stopped and slept in the car, but figured we'd freeze to death. Worse yet it might interrupt Honey's cycle.

"We have to go straight through," Jake said. "There's no choice that I can see."

"None I can see either," I replied. "You're doing fine. Keep it up and we'll drive out of this eventually."

When Honey complained Jake told me to let her out of her kennel, and she rode most of the way with her muzzle on the back of the seat between us. She whined now and then, eyes shining, that liquid yearning thing you see so real it could be human, and we took turns talking to her, naming the towns and telling her how far it was to Louisiana.

She hung in there, fine dog that she was, and when she met the Doctor it was love at first sight. I couldn't believe how it worked out. I mean, you can not expect things to go so well after the terrible day and night we'd had, but they did, and the result was now riding in the back seat.

"Jake, you can't expect Lady to be ready for this." It just came out, but it had to be said.

"She'll be all right," Jake said.

"It's new country. You can't expect a pup – even one as exceptional as Lady L – to bounce out of the box and do well when she's never even seen the Southland. She doesn't even know what the hell a woodcock is. If you turn her sour you will not be forgiven."

"And I shouldn't be," Jake said. "Guess I am pushing her some, but she's been ahead of *me* most of the way. Never had a pup so correct in every way. There were times it seemed like she *anticipated* my next lesson. You ever had that?"

"Not like you mean," I said, and felt a shiver. "And I don't know whether to feel relieved about that or not."

"She's the one, Ray. And then there's Q. Know what I

mean?"

For a moment there I could only shake my head. My God how many times had I heard this line from trainers that were normally sensible people. It wasn't that I didn't think Jake was dead on about Lady and the rest. She was an exciting pup to be around, whether you were just playing with a dummy or starting a lesson or going into a field. She would get the tremble in her shoulders, a tail quiver, but even at six and eight months she had this uncanny control, and yes, as Jake'd said, intuition. She knew things no pup should know. And yet she wasn't a pussy about it, which is something you have to watch for in setters that have the vision thing, pups which just come out with the full cellular memory that you always knew was possible, but just barely, and when it happens it is usually a temporary situation, a flash of brilliance that turns into hysteria. So the trainer pushes, the poor dog gets burned out or goes sour, and everything goes bad.

Competition does things to people. The best of it is when everybody feels the rush and loves their fellow competitors, like the knights jousting in olden times. But that sport went bad in the same way all sports do, when winning becomes more important than the game. Nowadays is no different. Back when I was an independent trainer I did not fully understand these truths, and for a long time I beat myself up trying to buck them.

That's why I help Jake now. He has a pretty good owner backing him. Not perfect, but there may not be a perfect owner, which are different from hunters who buy a finished dog. We call them owners, but really they're sponsors. I was present when this owner bought a stake in Lady L; that's unusual, but Jake wouldn't part with the whole pup or any say about how she would be brought into the game. He showed Lady to this owner and the guy went for the partial stake.

He liked Jake and the owner's wife liked Jake's wife and I figured this owner sensed Jake's sincerity and saw the pup was exceptional, a man who understood it can be better to be part of something great than own all of something less.

Jake hated to give up any interest in Lady, but somebody has to pay the tab so you can do your sport. Somebody has to have the desire and the money to pay for all the training and travel and lonely motel rooms, just for the chance to handle a beautiful thoroughbred that has the talent to be a winner. But really, what else is there for a part-time owner? Never knew one into whelping or messy early training or developing those rituals.

Besides, Jake had an ace going. He'd kept a dog from that litter, the biggest male. Named that dog Mister Q and swore me to secrecy. We trained these dogs together, but I knew Jake and Lori, his wife, also took them out. Several times when I drove up he'd be on the back porch feeding those pups little bits of granola bar. Jake wasn't a granola fan himself, but some young vet had told him they were good snacks for field dogs.

As for Q, he had every chance of becoming a top stud. He was built, cool and whipsaw smart with the papers behind him. And Lady was destined to be his promotional leader in the walk and shoot with an amateur handler. I knew Jake figured Q for all around within two years. If it worked out Jake would be set. Developing a top stud is about the best way to beat the financial anchor most trainers drag around.

"I believe," Jake said, rolling down the window, "I can smell it. Can you smell it?"

"Too soon. You're hallucinating."

"Now, Cory Ray, you know I have not imbibed drugs for many years. At least not illicit ones that inhibit mental capacity." When Jake was in a good mood he got a bang out of using fancy words he knew. He drew a deep breath from the air rushing in the window, turned to Lady who sat in so proper fashion on the rear bench seat, her freckled head almost between us; she had the clean black on white markings the judges like, classic hazely eyes.

"Smell it, girl?" Jake chuckled and reached to pat Lady's head. "Get that swamp and piney in your nose, girl. We're damned near to Lou-siana."

"It's nice," I agreed. "That crisp seasonal. You can't beat fall in the south."

We drove along for a time in silence. Suddenly Jake laughed into the wind pouring in the window, a laugh that burst out like birds exploding up right at your feet and it put me on edge.

"I've been geared for this hunt for about as long as I've been able to count the holes in my underwear," Jake said. "Did you know, Ray, I buy 'em that way now, have them ordered in special." He laughed again and pulled Lady's muzzle over to his cheek and they snuggled.

"Even still a baby you can beat that dumbass shorthair of Lee's," he told her. "You will make that kraut dog look stupid." Jake grinned, then shot me a stern look.

"What! You don't think so?"

I shook my head. "How can you be serious about that old feud?" I wouldn't look at him. "Don't want to hear it."

"Garland," Jake huffed. "What the hell kind of name is that for a dog? Specially a kraut dog. Do you say, 'No, Garland, honey, look for the birdie over here?' Do you say, 'Garland it's okay to poop in the flower bed, Daddy will pick it up?' How come this dog can score damn near perfect in a trial and still chase a cat up a tree? You were there. You saw him do that. What the hell was that? I think maybe Lee does something to that weirdo dog to make him excel at trials.

Maybe it's drugs, I don't know, but something is wrong with both those wierdos."

"Jake . . . get a grip. You guys played high school football together."

"I know," Jake said, nodding, glancing my way but my eyes stayed straight ahead. "Don't I know. He was a receiver while I did the dirty work. All right, I know you often sided with Lee."

"I just try to pick out what sounds right."

"You sayin' it's too soon to put Lady up against Garland? You think it might back her up?"

"Maybe," I said carefully. "It's a push. Only you can decide if it's worth it. But Floyd will be there with his dog too. Annie's also a good dog. Seems like Lady could learn from both those hounds. Seems like soft lessons might be the right approach."

Jake didn't say anything for a ways.

"There's truth to what you say," he admitted. "Annie's a fine pointer. Seasoned. Pretty hold and a good marker. A little too aggressive on the retrieve, but overall a top finisher." He leaned back with his thick right wrist draped over the steering wheel, bushy brows bunched in a frown at the road ahead and beyond the road.

"We'll ease into this exercise," he said finally. "The main thing is to bring Lady along, right?"

I just nodded. Jake was into his own place now, anything I might say would just be a rebound board against what he decided to do. I reached back and gave Lady a scratch. She put her head on my shoulder. She had the curse of being born with great genes. It was not a responsibility I'd been personally saddled with, but I sure could sympathize with a hound that had them.

We checked into Jake's parents' place that night and the

next morning met the guys at a spot they liked. Lee seemed in good spirits, all quick blue eyes and red cheeks, which to me meant he was looking forward to tormenting Jake. Floyd looked the same; on the short side but wide and powerfully built, deliberate walk, the same patient, small-horse expression I remembered from the previous year. Floyd was a stabilizing influence in about any situation.

We considered the stubbled soybean and cornfields surrounded by a fall marsh, along one irregular edge a lazy creek, brown-topped cattails, a few pine and knarly oak. An old plank bridge was partly hidden in morning mist from the creek. A bobwhite called along the creek, deciding for us which way to head first.

"Annie leans left," Floyd said. "I'll flank that way and you guys can have the rest."

"After all those pancakes I need to be in the middle," Lee said. "So you big fellas can prop me up." He put a hand on Jake's shoulder and gave him the cagey grin. "You wouldn't refuse a helpin' hand, would you, Jake?"

"Last time I noticed you were more frisky than sensible," Jake replied. "'Less you mistook me for one a them judges you been suckin' up to."

We all groaned, Lee most of all.

A few clucks of encouragement and Garland and Annie charged out full of confidence and assumed positions, began working the pattern. Right away Lady had a problem. She started out with the other dogs, paused, nose working all over the place.

"Give me a second," Jake said, and went forward. He bent down and talked to Lady. Her ears twitched and she frowned at him, then she went uncertainly into a pattern. She had plenty of scent but wasn't sure what to make of it in this damp, mossy country. In her young life she'd only

trained on clay and corn and alfalfa fields with clean smell-
ing birds. She was at a disadvantage here where even the
drier parts are sandy and full of pinewood smell.

"Well, look-e there," Lee announced. "Garland's got position already."

"Annie's on too," Floyd said. "I'll go wide."

Lady watched the shorthair and other pointer tensely
track forward, heads ridged. For the first time in her young
life I saw Lady look confused. Brow a series of ridges and
ears cockeyed, she moved toward the other dogs, nose working but not sure, posture all wrong. Suddenly she plowed
ahead and too soon a covey of about a dozen quail thundered
up. Shots were fired and two birds went down.

Lee was the first to yell *"Claim."* I didn't claim because I
was sure I'd missed the bird I'd aimed at. It was a long shot.

The three dogs went to retrieve. Annie and Garland each
delivered a bird. Lady sat down a little away from us, head
down, just staring at the ground. She hadn't even tried to
mark. Looks were exchanged, but nobody said anything.

It turned out to be a tough day for Jake and Lady. Jake
had some talks with her and didn't get too impatient, but
you could see he'd expected more. I guess Jake had such
great expectations he forgot she was still just a pup. I hoped
it was that more than the thing between him and Lee.

We put up a lot of birds. Quail in the morning, then into
the real wet stuff after lunch where it was mostly woodcock.
Lady had started to improve a little until we hit the swamp.
She didn't give up, but the long billed woodcock was a brand
new thing. They may smell and flush like a game bird, but
their feathers are oily and hair-like, a taste like duck I suppose, repellent to an upland bird dog from hard northern
fields.

By the end of the day Lady just looked lost. When Jake

fed her out in the backyard at his folks' place she didn't take it all. He'd turned down Lee's invitation to go to the rib joint, as well as his parents' offer to feed us, so we went to a diner down the road and had Salisbury steak and biscuits. We confined our conversation about the day's hunt to Lady's improvement in unfamiliar country.

When we got back, Jake went out in the backyard to spend some time with Lady. I went in to visit with his folks. After a time I noticed movement outside the front window, realized it was Jake and Lady walking along the gravel road in the twilight. It was cool now and still, a cool night that wouldn't frost and I thought the coolness might help Lady in the morning. Then I remembered something Lee had said about keeping them in the wet stuff so they'd be in shape for the first two shows, which were in Alabama.

The next morning we started right off with woodcock in a marsh next to where a small river eased out wide and bordered a farm where Jake said he'd worked summers during his school years. It was a nice birdy area full of little piles of slash and stubble that now in the wet season ran right down into the marsh where there was sweet gum and a few swamp oak. We got up birds in twos and threes all morning, missed a lot as you will on woodcock, or for that matter bobwhites that have been hunted so that they come out very fast and darty and hold low over the cover so your window for a shot is perhaps two seconds. It was good for us to sharpen our eye and swing over these very spooky birds.

Lee was the only one who seemed to connect about every time, yelling *"Claim,"* after every flush.

Jake began to wince every time he heard Lee claim. That and the fact Lady continued to have a hard time seemed to be working on him. A couple of times he even raised his voice to the dog. The second time this happened Lee said he thought Lady was doing real good for a pup in the wet for the first time, but Jake just turned abruptly away.

Lee's big blues widened into dramatic circles and he looked around at the rest of us, shrugged.

Jake seemed relieved when we called it a day right after noon. I know I was, and it had little to do with the quiet rain that began falling. We headed back to his folks, windshield wipers at four-four beat, not talking, which was fine with me. This was something Jake had to work out to his satisfaction or ruin. I knew he had the ability to see it through and not push the dog so she'd lose confidence. Still, you worry about those things.

That evening the rain stopped and Jake and Lady took their walk again. I slipped out on the porch and watched as man and dog moved slowly into darkness along the hedgerow that bordered the country road. It made me think of some times with my own dogs, just being together with the soft twilight sounds at the end of the day. There would be work tomorrow and the day after and you hoped it would go well. But then, in that quiet time, it was just nice to be together without the work or any interference.

The following sunny morning we started out in the wet again. There was a nice weed patch with some wild corn angling through flood ponds, channels dissecting it here and there, dew glistening on yellow and brown slash. Could be any type of bird in there. At first I just eased along enjoying the weak warmth from the rising sun. But I knew there was a difference this morning, this being the third morning and the first trial less than two weeks away. There was another dog over in Alabama Jake had promised the owner he'd help get ready. We would have to start east in a few days. Time to get down to business.

Lee was the only one still joking around, trying to get a

rise out of Jake, but Floyd's brow was a little more serious and the dogs, you know, they sense these mood changes in the people. They came out of their kennels ready for something; Annie more serious, Garland looking downright mean, and Lady with a look I hadn't seen since we left Illinois. She took her position in the middle, in front of Jake, paused with her nose working.

It was a good beginning. The dogs synced up as they set off running the pattern, ignoring each other but aware always of where the other dogs were, overlapping each others' pattern just right. These dogs were happy hunting together and it was pretty to see. They all made scent within minutes and went on it, heads ridged, moving slowly forward with Garland and Annie angling inward toward the straight line Lady was drawing.

All three dogs pointed. They were lined up almost perfectly. We moved in. Quail thundered up, cutting curly cues in the air. I was too excited to shoot, but the others did.

I heard Lee yell *"Claim."* I watched Lady make a perfect mark and find and retrieve to Jake. Annie and Garland did the same for the other guys.

Floyd tucked a bird into the game pocket of his jacket. "Well, that was something," he said.

"Did you see Garland's form?" Lee asked, like an announcement. "Zero subtraction. Full points. My boy's headed for a re-peat."

"The hell with Garland," Jake said. "He won't hold up through Oklahoma."

"Whoa boy!" Lee turned on the silly grin and buggy eyes. "Do we hear some low class disrespect for the next champion? Could your wild ambitions be over-runnin' your mouth, Jake boy? Or is this just more sour grapes in reference to the season past?"

"Look at you, puffin' like an old lady," Jake said without looking at Lee. "You'll probably have to ride Garland through Oklahoma. Could be a consolation trophy for that, or you'll invent one."

"Okay," Floyd said, meant to sound like an interruption. "Enough swamp practice. I must have a hole in my boot. Let's move up to dryer pickin's."

I readily agreed and Jake and Lee shrugged.

"I'm for anywhere the sun might be shinin' brighter," Lee said.

We loaded the dogs and drove about ten miles to a place I'd never hunted before. It was perfect farm country with bushy fencerows, uncultivated sections with a mix of pine, softwood and a few high nut trees. A clean creek ran between asparagus, lush grass and freshly cut corn, through a nice weed patch and into the woods. There was a farmhouse and barn up on a distant hillside, but Jake said there was no need to ask permission, this being his cousin's place. He tied a gold ribbon to the pickup's antenna so his cousin would know the right people were hunting the property.

The air was full of harvest and woodsy smells. You couldn't have asked for nicer bird country. I figured Jake had been saving this place for Lady, when he thought she was ready. The dogs came out of their kennels all excited and ready to go, especially Lady, this being more like the terrain she was used to, and with scent everywhere it was hard to contain them for a proper start.We finally got them into a line and headed into the stubble. This was not the usual clean-cut field of corn where you get a few kernels and partial ears and some slash here and there. There were places where it appeared the whacker had been raised so some stalks were a couple of feet tall with more cover slash and broken ears left on the ground. It was excellent cover and food and the dogs went-on fifty feet into the field.

The three were holding perfectly as we moved up, but Annie got it into her head to be first -- any setter can have brain fade -- and she half crawled forward in slow motion until her nose was almost in the slash pile where all those wet noses were pointing. This being the third day, the dogs all on, it was a serious lapse. The birds held well, but the flush was still a bit premature.

"Claim." Lee yelled as the echos from the shots were still dying out.

"I'm not so sure," Jake countered. "If you're claimin' that bird that went over the creek, I believe that one is mine."

"No way," Lee said. "You may have shot first, as usual, but when I shot there was a puff of feathers."

"I didn't shoot first, but if you're so desperate you need to claim other people's birds, go ahead. If you need it that bad go on and take the bird. Lady'l deliver it right into your hand. Here she comes. Go on and take the bird." Jake stalked off, began reloading while facing away from us.

"Sure I will," Lee announced. He reached down and took the quail from Lady. "I shot it. I don't have any pause in takin' it." He winked at me then, but I shook my head and turned away, hoping Lee would get the message that the game had gone far enough.

We kept on with Jake refusing to even speak to Lee, although he did cast some looks Lee's way that I would not have wanted to be on the receiving end of. Our stance had adjusted to Lee on the far left and Jake on the far right with Floyd and me in the middle.

Lee kept right on yelling *"Claim"* on every flush while Jake glowered.

We moved uphill to a weed patch of yellow grass and wild grain. All three dogs went on scent and held at almost the same time. We moved up and a big covey – about two dozen quail – thundered up together and split, peeling off to the left and right. There was shooting and I emptied my double.

"*Claim,*" Lee yelled before anybody could say anything.

"You must be a damn magician then," Jake said.

I looked back to where Jake was standing a little behind the rest of us, even behind Lee, who was a little back from Floyd and me. Jake had his shotgun cradled in his arm and I realized he hadn't fired. Then I saw Lee's sheepish grin.

"A real horned owl magician," Jake said.

For a moment I didn't know what was going on, and when Jake repositioned his gun I had a wild thought he might shoot Lee. No one really knows the depths of old grudges except the people holding them. My next thought was that I wasn't close enough to either of them to do anything about whatever might happen.

Lee's sudden laugh gave me a start.

"You," Jake said, staring at Lee. "You're a lyin', backshootin', cheatin' sumbitch just like you always were – and that goes for your kraut dog too."

"My kraut dog . . ." Lee began and then just laughed harder. He laughed so hard he put his trap grade Browning down butt first in the dirt and slid down it until he was sitting in that field with just his head and shoulders sticking up above the grass. And he kept on.

"You –" he began, pointing at Jake. "You should see –" but he couldn't continue because he just kept laughing.

Jake did not seem amused. "All day you been clamin'," he said. "And you haven't fired a shot."

"Twice," Lee managed. "Just to show you how it was done. And you have to admit, wing shootin' has never been your strongest suit, Jake boy."

Jake turned his glare on Floyd and me. The ridged lines in his big face began to soften. A corner of his mouth flicked up and I took this as a good sign.

"Hey, Jake," Lee said. "Don't you think we know what's going on? You've never had a dog like this before. I think she's the one. Not all the way this year. But by next year or the year after she could be champion."

"So what the hell's all this flim-flamin' about?" Jake demanded.

Lee shook his head. Garland brought a bird and dropped it in front of him. The commotion had spoiled his release, but it didn't matter at the moment. Lee put a hand on the dog's strong back for leverage as he got to his feet.

"I had a talk with myself a couple years ago," Lee said, watching Jake. "We both know I'm never going to be all around champion. Garland may have the stuff to win a show here and there, but I don't take it seriously enough. That's why I kept the store. I'm in dogs for a good time and the money I make off stud. I'm not like you, never have been. But that doesn't mean I don't want you to win the big one."

"What's this bullshit now," Jake said, mocking, "I *want* you to win. Because I'm not *like* you. I'm just a little also-ran suckling the judges." Jake stepped forward. "History says this is just another one of your scams. You like to mess with people. You like to lie."

Lee maintained his smile while walking slowly toward Jake. He walked right up to Jake until they were practically nose to nose, except Jake was higher and wider.

"You always took it so seriously," Lee said. "Football and all the way to the dogs. You have this really boring serious streak that's gone to your dogs competing. So now you have a baby champion. And if you keep the pressure on maybe you can break her. Or maybe you just want to break me."

I looked at Floyd and he was already looking back at me, both of us hoping I guess that if things went bad the other might have a clue about what to do. But I was not reassured Floyd was the one to count on, standing there with Annie pressed against his leg in a similar state of confusion.

Then we were all drawn to the only thing in motion at the moment, which was Lady trotting right through the middle of everybody with a bird in her mouth. I'd seen her go after the far bird that glided into a thicket at the edge of the field. She was all business, holding that bird high. Coming right to Jake and holding that bird up for him to take.

Jake stepped away from Lee, bent and accepted the bird. Lady made a perfect release. She backed up a step and looked up at him intently, tail a-quiver, ready for his next command.

"Good," Jake said quietly. He hunkered down and stroked her back. Lady accepted this but became uneasy, eager for her next assignment.

"You think she can be champion?" Jake said.

"Sure as shootin'," Floyd said. "Has the stuff. Adapted to south country faster than any I've seen."

"I already told Jake I thought she had the talent," I said. "Guess he needed confirmation by more parties."

"I didn't mean for you to take it that way," Jake said. He looked up and I could see the anger had passed. "Lee might build mountains out of bullshit, but I sometimes build things up in my mind so they become the same thing. Maybe it is the competition. Maybe I care too much about winning. I sure wouldn't want to do anything to hurt this little dog."

"You won't," Lee said. "You won't because if you mess up that dog we'll kill you. Right boys?"

"Well," Jake said, rising, "if I do I'll deserve it."

"I'm layin' this out once for all to hear," Lee said. "It's

a one time offer. I'm buyin' ribs for everybody at Smitty's. Now don't anybody feel obliged to accept, you can –"

"We'll accept," Floyd cut in. "And I'm real hungry."

Lee laughed. "Don't assume you can speak for everyone."

"He does speak for everyone," Jake said. "And beyond that," he winked at me, "it seems appropriate that the asshole's been claimin' all day without hittin' any birds –"

"I hit one!" Lee said.

"As I was saying," Jake continued. "The asshole's been lyin' most about his shooting should have to clean most of the birds before we go to Smitty's."

"Now wait a minute," Lee began as we started back for the truck. "Jake, now, you can't ask the man who's going to pay for your meal and good time to also do the menial work. There has to be some consideration for monetary outlay. It's the American way."

"In Lou-siana we're all commies," Jake said. "We want you to pay and also do the work."

"Your own momma would have a heart attack if she heard you say that."

"My momma would whip your ass for false clamin'. And I just might tell her about it."

"Now, Jake, don't go that way," Lee said, following along at his side. "We need to talk about this. Jake . . .?"

I watched the dogs marching ahead. Swinging their heads, testing the wind. They would hunt right up to being kenneled, not wanting to leave it. They were all fine dogs, but the pup stood out. She had the smooth confidence and the love. It was beyond anything a human could teach. Just watching her now gave me a warm feeling and I knew how much she would mean to Jake when the trials began.

RUN FOR YOUR LIFE

A sort of essay

At first I did not know he was marked for death, only that he had the saddest eyes I'd ever seen. He was tall and tan with the body of a cheetah and the head of a jet fighter. But those accepting, sad gold eyes changed the whole concept. I reached slowly to touch the top of his head, stroked the short, fine fur. Slowly his eyes closed. It was the nearest I'd ever been to a greyhound.

"Shouldn't mess with him."

I looked up at the service station owner. "Because he's one of your racers?"

"Not anymore," Neal said sternly. "He's on his way to Craig Allen's and a bullet in the skull. It's check-out time for Prancer."

The bell rang signaling a car out front and Jim, who worked for Neal, went to pump some gas.

"Why?" I asked.

"*Why*?" Neal turned from the cash register with his usual

scowl. He moved like a haystack grizzly and wore belliger-
ence as a symbol of honor, a multi-faceted businessman who
owned a two-pump gas and repair and bred and raced greyhounds in Denver in the mid-50's. The world was grappling
with a new concept called a Cold War, which by implication
meant if it became a real war we'd all be vaporized by nukes
right after the bright light blinded us. It had only been a
couple years since the government somewhat sheepishly
owned up to admitting that having school kids practice hiding under their desks if they saw a real bright white light
was a waste of time – if you were close enough to see it you
might as well utter a quick prayer before being hit by the
200 mile an hour wind from the blast. Jobs were scarce and
there was a recession about everywhere except California,
which at the time my age group thought of as the land of
milk and honey blonds and rods with enough power to set
fire to their tires - in other words paradise. They said in
California they had this stuff called smog you had to breathe
instead of air, but with all that upside everyone wanted to
migrate there anyway.

Neal considered the dog for a moment, his condemn-
ing gaze causing Prancer to shrink back. "Thought he'd be
a good one, but he can't get the speed. Can't knock off that
last couple tenths that would put him in there. Spent good
money tryin' to bring that dog up."

The bell dinged and I lurched to my feet. "I'll give Jim a
hand," I said. Neal nodded agreeably as I made for the door.
He always welcomed free labor.

Later, as we cruised toward the drive-in in Jim's leaded
and lowered '41 Ford, I asked why Neal didn't check around
to see if somebody could take Prancer instead of killing
him.

"Who'd want 'em?" Jim said. "Hey, these aren't like regular dogs. All Prancer knows is killin' and racin'. That's the way they're trained from puppies."

I tried to understand this line of thinking, but not for long.

"Hey man, don't be shaking your head all contrary. You bother Neal enough with that weird dog of yours and all those damn questions."

"Doesn't make any sense," I said.

"*Bullshit.* What do you know anyway? You heard how he trains 'em. Puts 'em in the fight box with a cat when they're only five months old. They want to see six months they have to kill the cat. Then they get a rabbit in the box. They have to kill rabbits and cats till Neal is convinced they have the instinct. Blood has to flow, man. He told you straight out, when they're properly trained he wouldn't turn his back on one. You can't put a dog like that in a home with kids and regular pets."

"Yeah. I don't know." I recalled how Neal had said proudly he wouldn't turn his back on one of his dogs after it was trained. "Doesn't make sense."

"Whad-ya mean – doesn't make sense? What *sense*?" Jim demanded.

"I've met one," I said. "And he wouldn't kill a person."

"Yeah, you're probably right – and that's why he's good as landfill now. A failure."

"Yeah. So who the fuck is Neal to judge that dog?"

Jim laughed. "Just a professional dog breeder and racer, that's all."

"I guess anybody can get some dogs and call themselves that," I shot back. "He couldn't get my dog eat that crappy food he makes till I said it was okay. And I'm not takin' that part-time job at the station."

Jim frowned over at me. "You gotta take it. Neal asked

you right out and you said you would. And when we get busy I need the help."

I didn't answer.

"Don't tell me it's on account of the dog! A racer too slow to make the cut that you don't even *know* or have a clue about the race business. Don't *tell me* it's the dog. Where else you going to get a job? There's no jobs to be had!"

I shrugged. What Jim said was true, I really needed the work. I was a seventeen year old school dropout with living expenses and a hundred dollar car that needed gas if you expected a girl to ride in it. The station was only two blocks from where I was living and it would be a little money till a real job came along. It wasn't that I expected to like the people I worked for – it was a bonus if it happened. But I guess my dislike for Neal had hit a blunt chord, become more personal. That Jim would think less of me or Neal might get on him because I wouldn't take the job wasn't enough to change my mind.

Around the time this was happening in Denver, Justice August Jones, who presided over a mid-sized spread just south of Amarillo, Texas, pulled his lanky form fully erect in the middle of his shadowy living room and announced he was going to drive all the way to New Mexico and buy a couple dogs. His wife, Florine, more or less pronounced him insane on the spot, but the next day he left for that lateral state. A few days later he returned with three of the strangest dogs anybody around there had ever seen.

Huddled in the back of his old stake farm truck, they looked out at the curious strangers and dusty new world they'd been delivered into. The dogs were fearful and thirsty and Justice had to hang on tight to their rope leashes to get them into the pen where he used to keep 4-H hogs before his daughter moved on to saddle horse competition.

"Looks like snakes with legs!" the oldest boy yelled.

"Those things ain't real dogs, Pa," the next youngest male said. "Are they?"

Justice was too busy to answer at the moment, wasn't even sure what the correct answer might be, but he had a coyote problem and a jackrabbit problem and a family to care for, and by God if these critters couldn't help solve those first two problems he wasn't sure what to do next.

Driving through that part of Texas, if the wind isn't being too mean, the country looks plenty sparse, arid, quiet except for the odd rolling storm or tornado. If you gaze out across the mesquite and creosote bushes, the odd teetering prickly pear, squint through heat waves present most of the year, you would probably conclude the whole flat land is barren of life. You can start walking toward a knoll about a mile away and soon enough realize it's farther away than you thought, and even sooner learn to avoid the squat cactus balls and Spanish dagger. And you will see the land isn't really flat but full of gouges, brushy arroyos and jagged canyons gouged out by flash floods, lightning, 200-mile-per-hour tornados. Near one of the scattered ranches you may pass a cistern made to retain some of the precious water that falls suddenly, hard, and as quickly disappears.

Ranch water has made life easier for the wild creatures, but they also know how to find natural water in the low places. Down in those ravines are miniature caves and small shady areas, and in those secret places are cool, sandy containers which can be scratched to find clean water – there isn't much water in the rocky pockets under the sand, but there is enough. In these low places most of the animals and reptiles that live in what is essentially a prairie desert spend their days. At night they seek food. After their hunger is satisfied, they multiply.

The year Justice Jones brought his snake dogs home the ranchers in that part of Texas were enduring tough times and the Jones' ranch was comparable to most; skimpy browse except in the first blush of spring, just enough to sustain his modest herd of sheep and two dozen head of cattle. Besides being at the mercy of the weather, the coyotes had multiplied on an easy diet of mutton and were killing three-quarters of his spring lambs and calves. Night patrols barely fazed them. They were too fast and elusive and in the dark it was impossible to shoot accurately. Hunting coyotes with a pack of foxhounds was hopeless. The wild dogs had become so prevalent and bold they regularly dug under the fence of the Jones' chicken coop only 50 feet from the main house.

Then there were the jackrabbits. They seemed to be on an up-cycle with the coyotes and consumed so much browse the sheep were ranging further and further to get enough to eat, which played right into the coyote's interest. What was a hardscrabble existence at best had become a life and death struggle. Some would say, Why not move on, settle in more hospitable country? People who talk like that are not farmers or ranchers.

Justice Jones had only seen pictures of greyhounds. Never thought much about it one way or n'other. Didn't concern him, wasn't a ranch dog. Heard they raced them somewhere. Then he saw an ad in the farm journal. Startling claims. He read it over several times with his finger underlining each word. A man in New Mexico was selling (*adopting* it said, but you had to pay) greyhounds that had been used as racing dogs. The ad said these dogs could run down a coyote.

Justice Jones was skeptical. No dog alive could catch a coyote on its own turf, and even if there *was* a dog that had the speed they could never outlast a full-grown coyote if it had a head start.

But Jones was desperate, so in his slow, printing hand he composed a letter and sent it off to the man in New Mexico. Three weeks later an answer came. Jones read the letter several times, pondered, counted the money he had left in the jar under the floorboard in his bedroom. Then he checked the oil and cleaned the spark plugs in his old truck and tried to think of some alternative to driving all the way to New Mexico.

He hadn't been able to figure any alternative. His decision had been reached through the same kind of logical, step-by-step thinking he'd used to determine it was time to start counter plowing. Water was scarce and getting scarcer. Had to make the most of what you were given. His neighbors didn't think much of the circles his plow made, some even joked about it behind his back. But that was five years ago and those that had laughed loudest were gone.

The sun dropped below the western horizon and Jones lit the lantern in the kitchen. He studied the list of instructions the man in New Mexico had given him regarding the care and feeding of his racing dogs. The man had emphasized the importance of obeying the list. His wife still thought he'd gone over the edge, but at least his five children had quit making jokes about the dogs. He looked out the window and saw three of them in the pen with the dogs, horsing around, the dogs dancing tall on lean hind legs and seeming to have a good time with his children. When they stood up like that they reminded Jones of his own sparse profile, and he smiled thinking how they might look in jeans and cowboy boots. Odd, the way these dogs didn't try to jump the fence and didn't bark when they played. The man in New Mexico had said they were good with well-behaved children. As far as Jones knew his children were better behaved than most.

It must be true because the dogs and his kids hit it off right away.

Two weeks, the man in New Mexico had said, three's better. These are ancient dogs with ancient ways. Don't ask anything of them right away. Let them ease in, get a little used to you and your family without a lot of excitement. They don't like turmoil. Then let them chase the lure.

After a week Jones began to feel some agitation. He needed those dogs now.

In his clapboard barn Justice found the long pole used for hoisting parts up to the windmill when it needed repairs. He tied the lure to the end of the pole with a short piece of rope. The lure was just a foot long wooden dowel wrapped in a rag with a few rabbit fur appendages.

His two oldest boys positioned the dogs on rope leashes and Justice began to twirl the long pole by moving it hand over hand over his head. The lure swung in an arc a few feet off the ground, moving fast at the edge of the wide circle described by the twirling pole.

Jones got the lure moving even faster and then nodded toward the boys. They released the eager dogs. Three seconds later Justice Jones was on the ground, having lost his balance when the first dog grabbed the lure. He wasn't sure what had happened, but he was impressed.

Jones repositioned the dogs and repeated the lure game with similar results.

Early the next morning Jones's oldest boy came in with news of another fresh kill. Two more lambs. Jones sharp jaw sectioned out like a ship's prow. He loaded his snake dogs in the back of the truck and with his two oldest boys set out to survey the carnage.

By the tracks if looked like three coyotes. They'd devoured their favorite parts of the two lambs where they'd been cut down. No need to drag them off, there was no competition from anything except other coyotes and there would be no pursuit worth worrying about. Tracks angled off toward an arroyo Jones knew contained shade.

"Shall we put those dogs on the trail?" his oldest boy asked.

Jones shook his head. "They're not trackers."

They followed the tracks as far as they could with the truck, stopped and got out. When the boys shut the passenger door, Jones saw a movement where he knew the edge of the arroyo to be, about 150 yards ahead.

Two coyotes stood watching them. Jones hadn't taken the rifle from behind the seat because he knew the moment the coyotes saw it they would disappear into the arroyo. If he so much as picked up a stick and put it to his shoulder the coyotes would dissolve into the prairie like a whirly-wind.

He looked back at the dogs. Three narrow muzzles were stuck through the bed stakes of the truck. Three sets of eyes were locked on the coyotes. No movement, no barking, just staring.

To the boys, Jones said quietly, "Don't move or talk."

He slowly walked back to the truck and considered the dogs. They quietly stared, their bunched muscles the only clue to what they might be thinking. Jones decided it was time to take a chance. He slowly swung open the tailgate. The dominant dog turned its streamlined muzzle and looked at Justice Jones. They held each other's eyes for several seconds.

"Go!" Jones said, then ducked as three dogs leaped over his head and hit the ground running.

It took the coyotes a few seconds to realize what was happening and by the time they turned the greyhounds had covered half the distance that separated them.

The boys were running after the dogs yelling "Pa! Pa! Look, Pa!"

Jones realized he was running too, saw the greyhounds streak over the edge of the arroyo and almost in the same instant three coyotes exploded out the far side, his dogs little more than a second behind. In moments two greyhounds flanked the closest running coyote with one directly behind. The coyote flew up in the air and was caught virtually on the way down, then another, and then there was just a dust cloud disappearing into the distance.

Jones puffed up to the first dead coyote and stopped. He panted, studying the wild dog, its sprawled position, as if it had landed dead. It was as if the coyote had taken a bullet in the brain while in mid-air. No predator killed like this. Nothing but a bullet or heavy club perfectly placed could kill like this.

"Pa!" his boy called, "Here's another one!"

"Pa! Pa!" the oldest boy called in the distance. "They're still runnin'!"

Jones found a smooth rock pushing up out of the prairie and sat down. "Lord, have mercy," he said. "I'm not sure what they are, but I'm grateful you sent 'em."

They soon came in without fanfare, three greyhounds trotting through dusty morning light with flecks of blood on their muzzles. Three quiet dogs that preferred to stand, though they had run flat out for as far as necessary to complete the job. The boys were petting and praising the two younger dogs. The tallest, oldest dog stood before Jones, mouth open a little, panting calmly. Jones reached out and stroked the short, fine hair on the head of a dog that was the result of over 4,000 years of evolution in the service of humans.

"That man who I got you from had lots of stories," he

said. "Didn't particularly believe a one of 'em completely, but I liked the one about the Greek feller, Odyssy or something. Had a dog like you, called Argus. Kinda like that name.

"Argus, let's go get you a drink a water."

And so it began.

Jones had one regular ranch dog left the coyotes hadn't killed, a black and white half-border collie-and-something-else. She answered to Daisy, was family dedicated and could track a little. Those tall, quiet, confident dogs intimidated Daisy, so they let her ride up in the front seat of the pickup, with the greyhounds and one of the boys in the back. In the cool, early mornings they drove rutted trails that passed for roads through the country they called home – and when they saw fresh coyote sign they put Daisy on it. She was a smart little dog and soon developed a bark that gave the humans an inkling of the age of the trail. Argus and the other two members of his team seemed to know at first bark what was going on and either turned back to whatever boy was in the pickup bed, or became very interested in what Daisy was doing. They would drive out on the prairie when possible, following little Daisy, until the game was spotted. Jones soon realized distance was moot. Unlike most dogs, his greyhounds had amazing eyesight – and the speed and endurance to catch anything on the horizon.

In a month of part time hunting the greyhounds killed sixteen coyotes and more than twice that many jackrabbits. Jones and his children skinned the coyotes and dried the skins over stretchers made of bailing wire. The boys rubbed in borax and wood ash to preserve the skins and make them pliable, turned the fur out, then the cured hides were given to a man who had a highway souvenir stand over on the edge of Amarillo to sell to people passing through. The jacks were cooked in a big blackened pot over a fire in the yard and the carcasses dried in the barn. Finally the meat was ground into small flakes and mixed with various combinations of steamed meal and corn; this became the dog's primary diet.

The hunting itself was an eerie process. Jones knew how wild canines killed, and he'd seen the result of dogs trained for the purpose, but these didn't fit anything in his experience. Jones was no longer sure greyhounds were dogs. These three had not been very familiar with each other before he brought them home, yet from the first they hunted as a team. They had been trained to compete solo in chasing a mechanical rabbit, yet they flanked a real rabbit running at terrific speed and one would reach in, like a surgeon making an incision, and snap the rabbit's neck. The rabbit would fly up in the air and be dead when it hit the ground. With coyotes, it usually required two moves – one snap to break a leg and send the animal flying up in the air and a second almost before it hit the ground to break its neck. One greyhound broke a leg, the other flanking on the opposite side moved faster than the eye could follow to administer the killing bite. He thought they would be limited in broken country, bound to be, those long, skinny legs would snap like dry branches while running over rocky, uneven ground.

But it made no difference. These animals ran like water over smooth rocks. No surface seemed to impair their efficiency. They closed on the prey with blinding speed and killed instantly. Once they were sure it was dead these so-called dogs would simply walk away, their job completed. A minute later they might be showing no aggressive behavior while playing coyly with his children.

There had been no training, Jones kept telling himself. That lure thing doesn't even count. They just know things. They simply know what we need them to do.

He took to sitting with them in the evenings when he was having his pipe, at first next to or in their pen and then, when he realized the pen was unnecessary, on the porch. Argus always took the first position at Jones' side, which gave the rancher an opportunity to study him.

One of the first things Jones learned was that Argus did not like his two cats. The dog would turn his head to avoid looking at them.

About a month after he brought the three dogs home, Argus killed a neighbor's cat that had wandered into the yard in search of the two cats that lived there. When Jones showed the dog the dead cat, Argus hung his head and turned his body so he was facing another direction. The only specific thing Jones knew about Argus' history was that he'd been born in Oklahoma and raced for three years while in his prime. Now, in this remote spread in Texas, his behavior was so perfect in every way, yet he could not abide the presence of a cat.

After some thought, Jones said, "Alright, Argus. I don't know what happened, but you don't have to put up with any extra cats. Just don't bother ours."

In the months and years that followed there were some that said Justice Jones had become obsessed with greyhounds. He was considered the local expert on the breed, although you would have to say there wasn't much competition. At one point he had on his ranch eleven of the dogs and seemed to spend an inordinate amount of time in their company. He began to hire out – usually on a trade-out basis, but if you were really strapped he'd hunt your land for nothing – to other ranchers who were being run out of house and home by coyotes and jacks. Jones occasionally sold dogs to people considered decent types that would take proper care of them.

In those times these elegant dogs were credited with saving many a farmer from ruin. This is fact. Unfortunately, some of the people who used greyhounds for this purpose were not as fair-minded or sensitive as Justice Jones. No one knew much about greyhounds and too often the people who bought them for predator control were the same kind who taught dogs to fight in makeshift rings called pits or boxes. The kind of people who have a need for cruel power over something. At the time, these dogs did not make fashionable pets. They didn't look right; too thin, tall, narrow, sat funny, skin problems (usually from the cages racers are kept in), oddly quiet, and when they did bark it sounded funny, like the first small yip of a coyote warming up to howl.

Curiosity took Justice Jones all the way to the town library, and the lady at the counter helped him find two books that told him more about his strange dogs, such as, several thousand years ago on the other side of the world it could mean a death penalty to posses a greyhound unless you were Egyptian royalty.

In the 70's a lot more people became aware of what was going on behind the scenes at dog tracks and breeding farms across the country. Not surprisingly, it was the most abusive racers who got the attention and, for a time, all greyhound racers were lumped into the same repulsive group. A growing number of outraged folks wanted to end greyhound racing, period. No changes, just stop. Their voices grew louder and louder. In an increasing number of states dog racing was outlawed. Desperate times for racers and track owners. They were facing extinction.

Three decades after Justice Jones made the trip to New Mexico and brought back the first greyhounds anybody had ever seen in that part of Texas, in 1987, the American Greyhound Council (AGC) was formed, a collaboration between the National Greyhound Association and the American Track Operators Association. From the beginning, AGC's mission has been, in their words, "to ensure the health, welfare and safety of racing greyhounds from the farm through retirement." The AGC is funded through a percentage of the purses paid at sanctioned races and matched by participating track owners. Strict rules were imposed for the care and training of greyhounds. The penalty for non-compliance is to be barred for life from any participation – even peripheral – in greyhound racing in the United States. The AGC got rid of some bad people and through concerted efforts helped to make some good new laws that benefit these amazing dogs.

Still, old habits die hard and it took the AGC and its initiators, the National Greyhound Association (NGA) and the American Greyhound Track Operators Association (AGTOA) until 1992 to ban the use of live animal lures in training, such as cats and rabbits.

Certainly among the AGC's greatest accomplishments are the education and grant programs that have fostered volunteer adoption groups in every corner of the country. Knowledge of greyhounds is usually matched by a growing fascination. These days nearly 20,000 retired greyhound racers are adopted each year to good homes. Many adopters decide they can take more than one.

Laws concerning the treatment of racing greyhounds continue into "retirement." It is illegal to hunt coyotes with greyhounds in most of the United States – the exceptions at this writing are Arizona and Texas. Justice Jones may still be in business down there at the base of the panhandle, but the greyhound laws in other places were never meant for him anyway. We all know that a new law usually is the result of a direct lobby for political votes, the distillation of mutual self-serving compromise, a literal sellout, even a turning of the sail toward a favorable wind. That's democracy, and it can have its beautiful moments. But do not for a moment think there aren't people in the business of breeding and racing greyhounds that don't love them for what they are.

Greyhounds are not like other dogs. They are canine ballerinas and they know it. Yet they were born with the disadvantage of wanting to devote their life to serving humans; it is in their genes and was instilled longer ago than you can possibly trace your family tree. No amount of abuse or crudeness can erase what became part of their nature so long ago. These dogs have known indulgence beyond the wildest canine fantasies, the pampered pets of pharaohs and royalty. They have also known terrible cruelty.

You could say they're just dogs, but don't say it to Justice Jones.

If you have an interest in bringing one home you should spend some time in the presence of greyhounds. Just be quiet and observe. Read a book, consider the sky, play a laptop game. When you look up they will be there, quietly watchful, ready to serve.

STATUES

I think we all have memories of individuals that have touched our early lives, and these people live in special files in our memory to be recalled when a particular sight or word or the evening sky reflected on slow moving water lets us see back into that time and marvel at the moment, and appreciate it so much more than we did when it happened. One of those people for me is the Statue Man. Not a lot of words passed between us, yet he was one of those amazements we encounter in life that leaves us with moon dust on our shoes and the absolute knowledge that there are people who transcend the ordinary while disguising themselves as completely and simply ordinary. When I think about him I always meld into the time just before we met and hear the clanking of train cars:

"'Aboard," was still ringing in my ears with Minaqua miles behind and my young eyes searching the passing winter-beaten fields, meadow ponds newly unfrozen, the edges and clearings of pine and birch woods for animals. The endless snow was good as gone, just white patches in shady places and dirty piles along the tracks, green popping out on bushes where there had been just a weave of frozen sticks, birds fluffing their feathers along fence rows like they'd just woke up – and there went two deer with flashing white tails bounding into dark safety under the trees.

Spring at long last.

Heading south with a one-way ticket to Wausau, sweet escape after the long, cold isolation in an unhappy house full of dangerous strangers.

They said it was the worst winter in thirty years – I believed it – and in that small house with a bare stud wall we held it back with a pot-bellied stove that huffed and sizzled every morning while I danced around trying to get my pants on. The furniture was on the other side of the room, away from the cold wall glistening with frost. On the wobbly coffee table a thermometer in the belly of a shiny metal fish read down to 20 degrees above zero, and below the black 20 was a peg where the needle rested every morning as Jimmy and I ate whatever food was set out. Stinging wind sliced my squinted eyes as I trudged snowy trails to school across the frozen lake, and during the wind's pause you could hear a door latch click a mile away.

There were times in the night I thought those people would kill me. I thought I'd never see my mother again and wondered if she even wanted to see me.

The violence became a kind of relief; after taking some verbal and physical hits there would be strange quiet with their shadows circling, as if you were in the center of a swirling storm, and I'd slink between those shadows and off to bed. I often peed in my bed and that set me up for the next round of punishment. But gradually I adjusted to my cold world and tried to make the best of it. I became more interested in the secrets of the woods, how to avoid frostbite and the defense of silence. And after walking the frozen lake every day and cutting wood after school, I was stronger and learning the power of physical violence since the discovery I could beat every kid in my class except Ray the Indian, two years older and much bigger. He was amused by my determination to put him on the ground. After he threw me down twice we became friends. Ray talked even less than me. Sometimes I'd talk for him, and no other kids dared bother us. School wasn't so bad after Ray and I became acquainted.

Miss Thompson, my teacher, a pretty blond lady, was always nice to me, although she gave me a D in dependability. I asked what that was and why I got a D in it, and she said it had to do with the fights I got in on the playground. Of course she didn't know what it was really like for a stranger out on that playground.

Then there was Corinne, which in the broadest sense you could call my first girlfriend, though of course she didn't know because I was too shy to tell her, or maybe she did know. Jimmy palled with her older brother and she invited me over a couple times on the weekend, her house about a half mile up the road, a really nice big house at the end of a long drive with bunches of sweet-smelling stock behind split log fence posts, giant red barn and green machinery everywhere.

Corinne and I played house. She had an elaborate handmade play house with all sorts of tiny furniture and little people who had complete names and particular jobs she assigned them. We walked around her farm some and she did most of the talking, which was fine with me, I just enjoyed being with the prettiest girl in class. I think she took my lim-

ited conversation as a lack of understanding, but she was
the first girl I'd tried to have something beyond childish conversation with. Her dad was nice enough, always busy, but I
knew her mother didn't like me much, giving me slant-eyed
glances while pretending to be quietly passing by. I was just
an outsider with no farm to back me up.

I thought I'd always remember Corinne and the lake in
front of the cold house where I'd learned to swim, but once
that train started moving I barely gave what was back there
a thought. It couldn't compare to what I imagined the future
would be.

My dog was in a cage two cars back, a caramel and white
border collie. The big-bellied conductor didn't like it much
when I made my way back to visit Skipper, some kind of rule
about kids in freight cars, but I told him it was necessary.
Skip had never been on a train or in a cage before and needed to know I was around so he'd stay calm and help quiet the
other dogs that weren't as smart and stable, like the barking
Airedale in a cage next to Skipper's. The conductor didn't
seem convinced, but he had a nice big face and kind blue
eyes pinched up by orange cheeks when he smiled, and I as-
sured him I didn't qualify as a kid anyway, having turned
ten already that spring. The conductor came to check on me
often and agreed Skip seemed to be a good influence on the
other dogs. I asked him about the gold chain disappearing
into a vest pocket and he showed me his official Hamilton
railroad watch. Told me it kept perfect time and wound it a
little while I watched.

My mother had taken a job with an insurance company
and she had a good place for us. Other people lived in the
big old house in Wausau where we had two rooms. There
was a man and woman that just got married and of course
the giant landlady who'd been a prison guard and had the

darnedest pair of little Boston terrier bulldogs. They were the first dogs of that type I'd been around. You never would think they could catch mice, being dogs in the strictest sense, but they were good at it. Almost every morning there would be a dead mouse or two laid out on the kitchen floor near the back door, little piles of grey fur and tiny pink feet. My mother wasn't as impressed with their hunting ability as I was.

These little mash-faced dogs sang right on cue for the giant woman, snorted and slobbered a lot and had strangely sophisticated eating habits, but I liked them and Skip was very patient with them, which is all you could expect from a real outdoor dog that also hunted. They say border collies can't hunt like regular hounds, but Skip had become a great squirrel dog just because I'd asked him to, as if he knew it was necessary. He could spot a grey squirrel flattened out on a limb at a hundred yards. Of course Skip was a dog genius, so it isn't fair to compare him with other non-hound dogs in regards to hunting skill, or any other skill. And although he always acted like a gentleman around people, Skip was a Northwoods dog and he'd just come through a winter of fifty below nights while sleeping in the unheated shop. I used to wake up in the cold dark and think about Skipper out there, wonder about sneaking him inside and taking the beating in the morning, but that was behind us now and here we were.

Wausau turned out to be a great place. My temporary school was only a block away. That school felt haunted it was so quiet. I didn't have one fight the two months I attended and even got good grades, including a B+ in dependability, although my teacher wasn't as nice or pretty as Miss Thompson.

Less than a mile the other way the Wisconsin River cut

right through town and me and Skip fished below the dam about every day, rain or shine. We didn't often catch anything, my tackle being pretty limited. When it was time to head home giant pike would be jumping out in the middle of the river, snaky silhouettes glinting in rosy twilight. I told Skip someday we'd have a boat so we could get out there and hang into a big one. We did catch several small walleyes and one northern pike more than two feet long.

On our way to the river we passed the Statue Man's house. There were about fifty sitting out on his lawn, real nice statues of birds and animals and miniature people doing various things like pushing a wheelbarrow or planting seeds. The Statue Man made them out of a kind of concrete right in his small shop next to his house. Some had color added and sticks and eyes and attachments made of wood or metal.

Skip and I often stopped at the Statue Man's house on our way fishing. He didn't say much, but he'd wave us into his shop and seemed happy for the company and sometimes he'd give us part of his snack.

I was amazed the way he'd take rodent wire and wood and jelly concrete and make a shape into a new statue. One time I asked where his plans were, and he tapped his head, a shaggy gray head with shiny blue eyes that often stared at something over in the corner or up on the ceiling. He didn't like you to talk while he was staring, but he didn't seem to mind me watching him work. I thought how great it would be to have a little shop like this and make things I liked and have people like them too and pay me to make more. I would ask the Statue Man the names of his tools – some he made himself – and he would ask if I'd caught anything the previous evening. Sometimes I'd be watching him make some nice new thing or telling him about my fishing adventures and forget the time and have to hurry to the river to get in a few casts before it was time to head home.

The day I caught the northern I stopped on my way home to show the Statue Man. It was nearly dark but he was in his shop working away under the bulb and wide brown shade that hung from the ceiling. He grinned when I held up the glistening fish.

"What'd you get him on?"

"Black and white daredevil. Right on top, too. I saw him hit. When I reefed him out Skip held him with a paw. Look at those teeth!"

The Statue Man gave a little laugh and reached for his tape measure.

That fish turned out to be a pretty big deal with the neighbors, since they were also fishing people. My mother got out her black Brownie Camera and took pictures with Skip and me and the fish. The next evening the giant land-lady helped us eat it and you know she got her share and then some. Even those little bulldogs got some of that fish, chattering and nibbling away.

A fever kept me away from the river for a few days, but then on a late Thursday afternoon I grabbed my fishing pole and headed out. On the way to the river I noticed the Statue Man's shop door was closed, so I started to walk on by.

Abruptly I stopped and stared. There was a new statue in his yard. I looked down at Skip, then back at the statue.

"Skip, it's us," I said. There we were more than half size, me with my fishing pole over my shoulder the way I carried it, Skip at my side with ears listening. Even without color he was a fine-looking dog. It was something to see us that way in concrete. Even my hair looked combed.

When I got home I told my mother about the statue. The next afternoon she and the giant landlady and one of the neighbors went down to the Statue Man's house to take pictures. All these people descending on the Statue Man was pretty embarrassing and I hoped it wouldn't mess up the relationship Skip and I had with him. Of course I wouldn't go with them. I didn't want the Statue Man to think I'd blabbed and got all these people to go down there and bother him.

But when they got there the statue was gone. The Statue Man told them it had already been sold, but he was considering making a couple more. Thing was, he'd told me he wasn't keen on duplicates of his own original concepts. He made a statue, that was usually it, not likely to be another one exactly like it. But in this case he was considering making a few more of Skip and me because of the interest the first one had generated. He had some custom orders that would keep him busy for a time, then he'd probably make some more.

This didn't make much sense, yards all over town with statues of me and Skip going fishing. Sure he was a handsome dog, but this didn't come across that well in concrete, and me, well, I didn't consider myself a statue worthy type. I couldn't understand why anyone would want us in their yard where they'd have to look at us every day. Due to my reservations about being a concrete decoration it was several days before I approached the Statue Man.

"I liked us in concrete. You got Skip down real well. But it's got everybody in an uproar because they can't take pictures because it's gone already. And you say you're going to make more when you usually don't. I just can't understand why anyone would want us on their lawn."

The Statue Man put down his big file. "Are you going fishing tonight?"

"Well, yeah." I adjusted the pole on my shoulder. "It rained today. I think we might catch something below Picnic Island. Or maybe at the point. This is a good time to try."

"It is because of what you think about fishing that I made

the statue. That is why someone bought it. And Skipper there, he believes too. When people see that, they want the statue so they can look at it every day. Here, I have some extra cookies."

I accepted two cookies, oatmeal, tasty lumps, slipped Skip half of the first one.

"But why is what *we* think important?"

The Statue Man chuckled in his relaxing way. "Not that exactly. It's what you believe is possible. Look." The Statue Man indicated his latest unfinished creation. "Do you see a swan?"

"Sure. A beautiful swan like I've seen on the river over where they nest. A swan in trouble it seems like. It has to protect its house, or maybe its young."

"Um. Do you suppose it will do that?"

"Sure it will, look at that beak. Those wings could knock out a dog. This is a tough swan for sure."

The Statue Man's eyes smiled at me and he looked back at his creation. "Yes," he said in that quiet way. "This *is* a tough swan. That's the finish I needed. This is going to be one tough ol' swan."

He laughed, and I did too, and then he went back to work. His mouth made expressions when he worked. Sometimes he hummed. He sure knew how to use those tools.

I watched the statue man for a while, then Skip and me had to head for the river. It had rained and there was a chance of good fishing.

THE AUTHOR AND MAC

Lightning Source UK Ltd.
Milton Keynes UK
UKOW041822051212

203263UK00001B/3/P